· 84.

# HOUSING, TAXATION AND SUBSIDIES

*A study of housing in the United Kingdom*

# HOUSING, TAXATION AND SUBSIDIES

*A study of housing in the United Kingdom*

ADELA ADAM NEVITT

NELSON

THOMAS NELSON AND SONS LTD
36 Park Street London W1
P.O. Box 336 Apapa Lagos
P.O. Box 25012 Nairobi
77 Coffee Street San Fernando Trinidad

THOMAS NELSON (AUSTRALIA) LTD
597 Little Collins Street Melbourne

THOMAS NELSON & SONS (SOUTH AFRICA) (PROPRIETARY) LTD
P.O. Box 9881 Johannesburg

THOMAS NELSON AND SONS (CANADA) LTD
81 Curlew Drive Don Mills Ontario

THOMAS NELSON AND SONS
Copewood and Davis Streets Camden 3, N.J.

First published 1966

Printed in Great Britain by
Thomas Nelson (Printers) Ltd, London and Edinburgh

# CONTENTS

# FOREWORD

*by Richard M. Titmuss*

Until Professor Donnison and his colleagues began their explorations in 1957, generously supported in a spirit of free inquiry by the Rowntree Trust, the problems of housing had been generally neglected as a subject of academic study and teaching by most departments of the social sciences in British universities. There were a few exceptions, of course, but in so far as the subject penetrated into the lecture theatre at most universities it did so in a narrow, technical, descriptive manner. Housing as a commodity in the economic system was not seen to be very different from many other market commodities. Housing policy was thought to be about local government and 'the housing of the working classes' and an appropriate, though dreary, ingredient of instruction for intending social workers. In this climate of opinion, compounded of a curious mixture of theoretical expertise and academic aloofness, research did not flourish.

Nor was it stimulated by the government departments concerned, who lacked, and seemed content to lack, the most elementary data on housing obsolescence, the resources of private landlords, the effects of rent control, subsides and a whole range of economic and social factors. The British people and their political parties, uninstructed in the basic facts and unaware of the extent of their ignorance, continued to grapple with their housing problems in the vocabulary of a class-conscious folklore inherited from the nineteenth century. This encumbrance of myth and counter-myth affected opinion about landlord and tenant, the law of real property, the effects of rent control and decontrol, the definition, incidence, cost and distribution of housing subsidies, the demand and supply of new houses, and even the fiction in fiscal law that houses last for ever.

Since 1957 this situation has changed and we are now, in 1966, beginning to see something of the illogicalities and inequities that have come down to us from the past, and which have helped to shape legislation and policy as well as public opinion. For much of this destruc-

i

tion of myth (which is or should be a primary function of the university) we are indebted to Professor Donnison and his colleagues in the Department of Social Administration at the London School of Economics and at the Universities of Glasgow, Nottingham and Exeter. In the last eight years we have had from them a steady flow of books, papers and articles reporting and analysing the results of research undertaken on a national, London and local scale. They have helped to set us free from some of the myths and misconceptions of yesterday which are peculiarly liable to colour our attitudes and feelings about ' house ' and ' home '.

This book by Miss Nevitt, a member of the Rowntree Housing team, and one who contributed much to the work of the Milner Holland Committee, first by submitting research evidence and then as a temporary civil servant, adds further to our understanding of the real nature of the nation's housing problem. It does so—and this is its particular value—in the extraordinarily complex and difficult world of housing economics.

Why, as we become wealthier, does the problem of paying for adequate housing seem to have become harder for many families? Why are millions of families faced with a narrowing choice in methods of obtaining and paying for accommodation? What is the explanation of the apparent paradox that the decontrol of rents has led and is leading not to the supply of more rented accommodation but to less? How has it come about that many owner-occupiers are more heavily subsidized than council tenants as a group? What have been the long-term effects of the fact that not until this century was it legally possible for millions of people to own a small area of freehold land? These are some of the questions which Miss Nevitt examines with coolness and logic. She brings to bear on these questions much more than the analytical tools of an economist.

This breadth of approach is one of the signal merits of the book. To understand fully the problems of British housing it is necessary to understand the land-tenure system, the public-health laws which control the structure of houses, the housing laws which control their occupation, the laws regulating the relationship between landlord and tenant, the town-planning laws which control the location of houses, the fiscal laws which determine price, preferences and methods of paying for housing, and the roles that government and the private market have played in the housing field over the last hundred years. Miss Nevitt does not parade all her learning, but deploys that which is essential to give us a more comprehensive, historical explanation of the current dilemmas in the economics of housing. She helps us to see how the bits fit together; something that policy-makers, entrepreneurs and the public in general have not been assisted to recognize in the past. The doctrinal simplicity of the free market versus state interference thesis may now, we hope, lose some of its appeal. It has flourished for too long on the mythical gods of the nineteenth century and on a separatist, insular approach to the laws of land, housing and taxation. The distortions of price, subsidy, taxation and rent that now encumber us are more the product of uninformed absent-mindedness and pressure-group politics than of calculated wickedness.

This is not only a book which educates but one which ends with constructive suggestions for reform. In her concluding chapter, Miss Nevitt brings together the main themes of the study and outlines proposals for rationalizing the taxation of revenue derived from houses, for reconstructing the whole system of housing costs, particularly for those with less than average incomes, and, finally, for creating a financial institution to meet the need for loans of landlords and local authorities.

# ACKNOWLEDGEMENTS

This research is one of a series of studies carried out by the members of the Rowntree Trust Housing Study. The research has received very generous support from the Joseph Rowntree Memorial Trust and the author has been greatly helped by the Trust's Advisory Committee consisting of Professor R. M. Titmuss, Sir John Wrigley, Mr Lewis E. Waddilove, Professor François Lafitte and Mr W. B. Reddaway.

Very valuable assistance and advice was given to the author by her colleagues at the London School of Economics and the other members of the Rowntree Trust Housing Study who are working at the Universities of Glasgow, Exeter and Nottingham. The author has also been most grateful to the many treasurers and housing directors who kindly read some parts of the manuscript and greatly improved it by their constructive criticisms. It is impossible to name all those who have helped by reading the manuscript and making innumerable suggestions for its improvement, but particular thanks are due to Professor D. V. Donnison, Mrs Christine Cockburn and Dr Roy Parker. The author is, however, fully responsible for all errors of omission and commission and none of the individuals or organizations mentioned above bear any responsibility for the views expressed in this book. On a subject as controversial as the economics of housing it would be difficult to find any group of people in complete agreement as to the nature of the problems involved and their solutions, and an important aspect of the generosity of the Trustees of the Joseph Rowntree Memorial Trust has been their encouragement of the expression of opinion with which they do not necessarily agree.

# CHAPTER 1

# *Introduction*

Because of the many legal complexities which surround the subject, housing economics is one of the more difficult branches of applied economics. To understand British housing fully it is first necessary to study the British land-tenure system, the public-health laws which control their structure, the housing laws which control their occupation and the town-planning laws which control their location. The laws controlling rents and regulating the relationship between landlords and tenants add to the problems of students of housing and have led many people to believe that the only lasting solution to 'the housing problem' is the municipalization of all rented property. Despite the great temptation to write a book on one or more of these topics, this one has been entirely devoted to an examination of the financial aspects.

This concentration of material inevitably produces a certain lack of balance, and the reader must not expect the present work to produce any universal solution to our housing problems. That we have an acute shortage of houses in some areas of the country is evident from the statistics of the 1961 Census and the housing surveys carried out by the Rowntree Trust Housing Study in 1958 and 1962 as well as from the government surveys which were undertaken in 1960 and 1963;[1] but the number and condition of our houses is a symptom of our method of financing them, and until we fully understand the implications of our methods of financing, taxing and subsidizing them we cannot hope to arrive at any solution to our problems. The lack of bathrooms is, for instance, a direct result of our taxation of bathrooms. The decline (and if nothing is done about it, the ultimate disappearance) of the private landlord is again a symptom of our tax laws, which give his competitors, the building societies, such an economic advantage that the ordinary landlord can no longer compete with them.

1. D. V. Donnison, Christine Cockburn and T. Corbett, *Housing Since the Rent Act*, Occasional Papers No. 3, Codicote Press, 1961; D. V. Donnison, Christine Cockburn, J. B. Cullingworth and Della Adam Nevitt, *Essays on Housing*, Occasional Papers No. 9, Codicote Press, 1964; P. G. Gray and R. Russell, *Housing Situation in 1960*, Central Office of Information, 1962; J. B. Cullingworth, *English Housing Trends*, Occasional Papers on Social Administration No. 13, Bell, 1965.

The strength of the building society does not, however, rest entirely upon the unfavourable tax position of the landlord, but also stems from the nineteenth-century invention of the amortized loan. This invention is of such importance in housing economics that it should rank with the invention of the steam engine in changing the face of Britain. Owner-occupation and all the social changes which this implies only became possible when a method had been discovered and perfected of borrowing money over a short period and lending it out over a much longer period. The building societies are a natural extension of the commercial banking system of borrowing short and lending long, but the implications of this development, while being well understood by bankers, has been gravely under-estimated by students of housing. The statistics of building societies are now published regularly with the country's other financial statistics, but do not appear in such important places as the Ministry of Housing annual reports, although housing conditions now depend more upon the activities of the societies than upon any other single institution.

From a strictly economic point of view the great significance of owner-occupation is that it is a form of finance which involves the investment of capital without the payment of interest. Owners put their own capital into their own houses and gain a real income. This introduces a great flexibility into housing economics, and if all families were owner-occupiers it would mean that only about 50 per cent of all the capital invested in houses was paying an interest return. The rest of the capital sunk in the nation's housing stock would be the savings of individuals, each of whom was content to enjoy a real income from the savings instead of a money income.

As owner-occupation is enjoyed for its own sake, the incalculable economic advantage of financing houses by this method accords with our current social needs, and government encouragement of owner-occupation is, in the real democratic sense, a fulfilment of the wishes of the electorate. While, however, every encouragement can beneficially be given to owner-occupation, there seems no reason why other tenure groups should be neglected.

The nineteenth-century private landlord is no longer a viable economic proposition. Like so many other nineteenth-century institutions, the small private landlord is the victim of progress. Progress, above all, in financial institutions and organization, but also in town and country planning and social attitudes to public health and social welfare. Just as we may now nostalgically regret the passing of the music-hall, so we also regret the lost variety which the private landlord brought to the housing market. We are no longer able to choose a house from a great selection of different types of tenure and quality of accommodation. Most of us are now faced with the choice of either a freehold or a weekly council tenancy with the statutory right to four weeks' notice of the local authority's intention to evict.[1]

Eighty years ago families had the choice of good, bad, very bad and indifferent accommodation on tenancy terms ranging from the weekly tenancy granted without any written agreement, to the building lease of ninety-nine years. All these tenancies are still legally available and, regrettably, so are some of the very inferior houses; but relatively few families can exercise the choice which the law allows, because the supply of private houses to let is steadily diminishing. The narrowing choice has, however, been accompanied by a reduction in the cost of capital invested in houses. Today the average return paid on capital in houses is probably about 4 per cent and in the nineteenth century it was certainly 8 per cent and very probably nearer to 10 per cent.

The low average return of 4 per cent on the whole of the capital is only possible because owner-occupiers are content to invest their own capital without a money return and local authorities do not operate on a profit-making basis. In the past fifty years the possibility of having houses paying such a low return on capital has become so attractive that 70 per cent of all families are now living in houses upon which this low return is made. Despite the expression of some regrets about the loss of the private landlord, it seems very clear that those who still live in privately rented accommodation look with envy at the rest of society and would willingly exchange the variety of choice offered by the private landlord for the low price of the local authority or owner-occupied house.

The remaining 30 per cent of tenants represent, however, the 'hardcore' of the housing problem. They include, in disproportionate numbers, the old, the newly married, large families and in general the poor and the very poor.[2] The main hope for these people is that we shall find a way of bringing them into the low return on capital sectors of the market and also into the subsidy system, which already covers the other two sectors. We can do this by rationalizing the tax position of the landlord and actively encouraging landlords, or by incorporating the private sector with the local-authority sector.

As choice with cheapness is an important element in economic

1. The fact that local-authority landlords very seldom evict any tenant does not alter their right to do so.
2. Donnison, Cockburn, Cullingworth and Nevitt, op. cit., pp. 30–4.

well-being, it would seem a pity to allow the private landlord, particularly in the form of the housing association, to disappear completely. Local-authority building during the next ten years will no doubt raise the proportion of local-authority tenants from 30 to about 40 per cent, and a further extension of owner-occupation is likely to raise the proportion of owners from about 40 to 50 per cent. During the same period, housing associations might beneficially increase so that about 10 per cent of families lived in property belonging to associations. This would lay a firm foundation for a future expansion if the families of the 1975–2000 generation preferred housing associations to the other forms of tenure. If things are permitted to continue as at present, the next generation of householders will be left with the single choice of living in owner-occupied houses or houses owned by the local authority.

As we have now allowed the private landlords' economic position to be very severely undermined, there is little hope of making any improvement by a mere tinkering with one or two aspects of the unfavourable economic environment in which the landlord operates. The removal of rent controls or the introduction of a comprehensive and rational system of rent regulation cannot help either landlords or tenants unless the burden of tax is also lightened. The position is now so bad that, even if rents and taxes were reformed, it would still be necessary for the Government to give active encouragement to the creation of a capital lending institution which would specialize in meeting the needs of private landlords.

The new Housing Corporation may constitute the foundations around which such an institution could be built. In its present form, however, it is not very encouraging because of its very close association with the building societies, which are, very properly, dedicated to the extension of owner-occupation. There seems no good reason why the Housing Corporation should not borrow extensively from the Stock Exchange and the insurance companies. If the Government were to support its borrowing by granting a guarantee on interest payments, the Housing Corporation should be able to deflect funds from the construction of offices, bingo halls, hotels and other forms of investment which compete for the resources of the building industry. There seems no particular reason why the Government should grant a subsidy to the corporation, but until it is firmly founded a government guarantee of all interest payments would give lenders, both British and overseas, the necessary confidence to make large-scale investments.

Even if all these things were done to resuscitate the landlord, it would still not be sufficient to make his position economically viable. It would also be necessary either to remove subsidies from the other two tenure groups or to permit the tenants of private landlords to enjoy subsidy. Rational rent regulation, the removal of some of the tax burden, the supply of capital and the co-ordination of all subsidies must be seen as part of the same comprehensive housing policy. If any one of these financial reforms is neglected for lack of political courage, the other reforms would not be successful in increasing either the supply or the quality of the nation's housing and we shall be thrown back on owner-occupation and local-authority housing for a long-term solution to the housing problems of our towns and cities.

The arguments to support this view are put forward in Chapters 2 to 9 of this book. In Chapters 2 and 3 a brief account of the historical development of land tenure in England is given and an assessment made of the economic impact of both the legal and financial changes which have occurred since the sixteenth century. Chapters 4 and 5 deal with the taxes on rental income and the tax relief claimed by individuals in respect of interest payments. The sixth and seventh chapters give an account of the development of local-authority housing and relate the direct subsidies given to the tenants of local authorities to the levels of tax relief obtained by owner-occupiers.

In Chapter 8 the general effect of controlling and then decontrolling rents is discussed. In assessing the decontrol of rents by the Rent Act of 1957, it is particularly necessary to emphasize that the fault of this legislation was not that it sought to raise rents, but that it proceeded on the assumption that things were as they had been in 1857. So many of the important financial and fiscal facts of life changed between 1914 and 1957 that it is impossible for us ever to return to a nineteenth-century position. We must either invent new institutions and methods of taxing and/or subsidize tenants and landlords, or else we must face the full consequences of our inability to do so and accept the total disappearance of privately rented accommodation for the average family.

In Chapter 9 the relationship between the general level of income and the price of houses is examined, in so far as the available statistics will permit this to be done for the United Kingdom. In the last chapter of the book, a new method of subsidizing housing is suggested. The co-ordinated system proposed has been put forward because it seems to flow from the discussion and criticisms of the earlier chapters. It must however be emphasized that the last chapter is not an attempt to present a national housing policy. It is simply a proposal which should lead to a more rational and equitable distribution of government aid to housing. The long-term solution of our housing problems must rest on a far wider basis than the integration of fiscal policy with housing objectives.

Regional planning, industrialized building and the reform of the laws of landlord and tenant, conveyancing, and many aspects of the housing laws which control the use of accommodation must all play their part in translating the aspirations of the people into reality. The introduction of legal reforms and technical changes must however be accompanied by a thorough modernization of those of our institutions which bring capital to the housing market and allocate subsidies or impose taxes upon houses. It is for this reason that this book has concentrated upon these aspects of British housing and has ignored the many other facets of the problem which have already attracted so much attention in the Press and literature on the subject.

# CHAPTER 2

# *Rents and the Sale of Land*

Many of the present housing problems in the United Kingdom have arisen because we have been unable to find any socially acceptable method of keeping the capital value of accommodation within the rent or mortgage-repayment capacities of a large number of families. The majority of families in the country pay for their accommodation out of income, and the general level of income determines the general level of rents. Rents in turn determine the capital value of property, and it should theoretically be possible to move from capital value back to current rent levels without social or economic hardship arising for those who pay rent.

However, as the capital market is very flexible and capital prices quickly adjust to the expected future price or rent of something, the conversion from capital value to rental value during periods of inflation results in 'high' current rents. An example may make this relationship a little clearer. If the current market rent of a house is £200 a year, the capital value of the house will be about £3,300. If, however, the rent is expected to be £300 a year, in two years' time the capital value will rise to about £5,000, and if the house is sold a new owner will try to get the higher rental as soon as possible. This is because while he continues to take a rent of only £200 he is getting a very low return on his £5,000 capital. If the higher rent is obtained immediately, the capital market adjusts to the fact that rents are rising even faster than was at first thought and there is another round of increased capital values. Once this inflationary process has started it can continue for some time before the level of current incomes again asserts a dominance over capital values.

The process by which capital values catch up with and then pass above rental values is usually known as speculation in land prices and very commonly condemned. In this chapter the way in which the level of rents and mortgage repayments affects capital values is to be examined, because the inter-relationship of these two things is vital in understanding the problems which confront both the occupiers and the owners of property.

The relationship will be discussed with a brief historical mention of the English property laws, because only in comparatively recent years has all land been freely saleable. Land clearly cannot have a capital value if the law prevents its sale or imposes onerous conditions upon the seller, such as making him obtain a private Act of Parliament before he is able to sell the freehold of his land. Over the last four centuries, land has been gradually converted from a relatively simple rent-yielding asset into a capital asset which is priced in the capital market. Owner-occupation of a house is the end result of this change; to owner-occupiers rents have become of relatively minor importance, but the rate of interest and the length of a loan have become of overwhelming economic importance to them.

### Sixteenth-century development in land tenure

Up to the sixteenth century relatively little land was bought or sold in England. The property laws of the country were based upon the assumption that land did not belong to an individual but to a family or a corporate body such as a college, city, church, monastery or hospital. The land which belonged to a family was the property of both present and future generations of the family. The individual who happened to be alive and in control of an estate at any particular moment of time had no legal right to do anything to the land which would reduce the income of succeeding generations. As the children of such families could not defend their own interests, the law was designed to protect both the wishes of past generations which had bequeathed land for specific purposes and the interests of future generations.

There were many legal devices by which their interests were protected, but the most important economic device was a general prohibition on the sale of land. Leases for a period of lives could be granted, but these were limited in length and when the landlord granted a lease it produced an annual rental income for the landlord and not a large capital sum of money. Fines were imposed when leases were renewed, but the fines were usually fairly small and often seem to have been regarded as income in addition to rent rather than as capital for the sale of something.

In general these arrangements required a simple and fairly flexible economic structure of debts and contractual payments. Tenants had a yearly income from which they paid rent; the income was frequently measured in crops and the rents often paid in kind and not in cash. Variations in the harvest and the types of crops grown were reflected in the amount of rent paid, and, on the whole, rents and 'income' would tend to keep in step.

Under these conditions, relatively few people needed to borrow capital and even fewer people had capital to lend. Mortgages were certainly known and used, but it is doubtful whether they were for very long terms or, whether indeed, they amounted to much more than a loan given and secured on one or two years' rent income. In general, it may be said that the principle of mortgages was well understood before the sixteenth century, but the necessity for them was not very great.

As the economy advanced from the early rigid medieval structure merchants began to accumulate capital, and land became one obvious investment in which such capital could be placed. At the same time, landlords who normally had much land but little capital were theoretically able to obtain capital by giving up some of their legal interest in land. Financially this could be done by obatining mortgages, by grant of long lease, or by outright sale of the freehold.

The law effectively prevented the sale of the land freehold and landlords were therefore obliged to consider the long lease or the mortgage. On the other hand, investors who wished to obtain control over a plot of land were not much interested in mortgages which give the investor a minimum of control. Thus in the sixteenth century capital and land came together through an extension of the leasehold system of land tenure. This system satisfied the immediate needs of both investors, who wished to control the use of land, and landlords, who were willing to give up some of their rights over land in return for a substantial capital sum.

However, legal obstacles prevented any rapid fulfilment of the growing economic possibilities of making investments in land. During the sixteenth century these restrictive property laws were severely undermined but by no means overthrown by the confiscation of the monastic lands by Henry VIII. The attack upon the property laws came from certain abbots who had obtained some news of the king's intentions to confiscate their lands and hurriedly granted long leases of the monastic farms in return for high premiums.[1] Some of those leases ran into the seventeenth century, and as the lease rents were very low the Crown obtained little revenue or benefit from the lands until the leases fell in. The abbots were, however, enriched by the arrangement and the heads of other corporate bodies who were in no danger of having their lands confiscated followed the example set by their less

1. Stephen Dowell, *History of Taxation and Taxes in England*, Longmans, Green, 1888, 2nd edition, vol. I, pp. 136–40.

fortunate contemporaries. By 1558 the sale of long leases had become sufficiently common to receive parliamentary attention and an Act was passed to prevent bishops and other spiritual persons and the owners of settled estates from granting leases which exceeded twenty-one years.

This statute is an interesting example of an attempt to stop the rising tide of a new economic phenomenon. The sellers of long leases were specifically attacked and restrained by the Act, but as sellers can only exist in conjunction with buyers, the Act was foredoomed to failure. The only way in which Parliament could have put a stop to the activities of the buyers of long leases would have been to take away their economic power to purchase land. Far from wishing to do anything as drastic as this, the Elizabethans actively encouraged merchants to enrich themselves and the nation by foreign trade.

The Act is also of great interest today as it is an early example of legislative attempts to control the level of rents. Unlike twentieth-century rent-controlling legislation, this Act prohibited the reduction of rents but permitted rents to be raised. An economic justification for this provision is that, when rents are high, lease premiums will be low. Or, in other words, if the rent which an occupier must pay is kept high, the capital sum which the occupier is willing to pay will be low.

The 1558 Act was therefore a direct attempt to stop the capitalization of land. Parliament's main intention was almost undoubtedly to stop the impoverishment of the Church and other charitable foundations. If the present incumbent of church lands was permitted to sell a long lease at a fixed and extremely low ground rent, those who succeeded him to the living would have had to live on the low rents and they would obtain no benefit from the capital sum paid for the lease. By prohibiting leases which exceeded twenty-one years Parliament removed one incentive for giving a large capital sum for a lease, and by imposing minimum rents it intended to remove the other incentive for paying lease premiums.

This control over landlords and tenants must have been particularly onerous when tenants wished to build upon the land they had leased. As a house lasts for more than twenty-one years, few tenants can be persuaded to create new buildings under the conditions imposed in 1558. In 1572 Parliament gave recognition to the special needs of such tenants and the law was altered to permit the grant of forty-year leases in cities, towns and suburbs if buildings were to be erected on the land. The Act of 1572 therefore recognized the needs of tenants but did not give very active encouragement to them. Rents were not to be lowered and thus lease premiums were still kept low.

For two reasons this Act was not very effective in preventing the sale of leases. First, the sixteenth century was a period of inflation, and as it was the "accustomed" rents which had to be charged by the law, these old rents would gradually have fallen in value and must finally have become a relatively insignificant factor in negotiating leases. Secondly, the law was very widely ignored.

Throughout the seventeenth century the legal limit of forty years was either ignored, or private Acts were obtained which authorized leases of sixty to ninety-nine years, and it was not until the beginning of the nineteenth century that the long lease received statutory recognition as a normal method of land development. The authors of the report on *Residential Leasehold Property*[1] assumed that the length of a lease was related to the expected life of a house. There seems little economic reason for making this assumption and there is no empirical evidence to support their statement that '99 years used commonly to be chosen as a suitable term for a building lease, in the belief that the buildings to be erected would not last longer than a century, and the property would then need to be redeveloped'.[2]

The length of the lease seems on the whole to have depended upon the bargaining strength of the two parties involved. When it was necessary to encourage an increase in building, as, for instance, after the Great Fire in 1666, building leases tended to lengthen. When land was in short supply landlords could get builders to accept shorter leases. But the general trend of development was towards a lengthening of the term. In the seventeenth century the term in London was forty-one or fifty-one years, and during the eighteenth century it increased to sixty-one, eighty-one and finally ninety-nine years. Many of the leases were of doubtful legality and the London teaching hospitals rushed a retrospective Act through Parliament in 1825 legalizing their leases when one of their tenants queried the validity of his lease which contravened the Acts of Elizabeth I's reign.[3]

*The difficulties of converting land from a rent-yielding asset*
*to a capital asset*

As the legal and economic difficulties associated with the sale of land were gradually overcome, the position of the landlord in society declined and that of the lender of the capital became of greater importance.

1. *Residential Leasehold Property*, Ministry of Housing and Local Government, Cmnd 1789, July 1962.
2. *Residential Leasehold Property*, op. cit., p. 4.
3. Mrs Brenda Swann, 'A Study of some London Estates in the Eighteenth Century', unpublished thesis accepted by London University, 1964.

As soon as the 'occupier' of land has to pay a capital sum equal to from fifteen to thirty times the annual rent income of the land, the need for a lender of money becomes fairly obvious. The moneylenders constitute an essential bridge between sellers and buyers and it is fairly certain that in the sixteenth century there were too few lenders of money to allow a great many landlords to sell their lands without lowering the price of land. The parliamentary choice of forty years (in 1572) as the maximum length of a building lease was no doubt partly determined by a custom which had developed of granting leases for about this length. It is only after financial institutions have been developed that the freehold unencumbered estate can be sold with as much ease as a forty-year lease.

So far a capital market has been referred to as if, like landlords, lenders and borrowers formed clearly defined social groups. In fact the terms lenders and borrowers are economic categories and not in any sense social groupings. The growth of methods of marketing capital has been determined almost solely by economic needs and criteria.

In very general terms rents are set with reference to the capacity of someone or some institution to pay the amount asked. Rent differs in this respect from other prices, which are set by the expenses incurred in making the article. Rents are always paid out of income, and for property such as shops or offices the firm with the highest profit income offers the highest rent and obtains the letting. The same principle applies in the case of residential property: families with high incomes offer higher rents than those with average or low incomes, and the richer families therefore obtain the limited amount of accommodation available in places like the West End of London. Families with average incomes offer smaller rents for accommodation which is less favourably situated, and since incomes tend to cluster about the average, the rent of a great amount of accommodation tends to be within the means of many families. Rents are, however, set with reference to average incomes, which necessarily means that those with less than average incomes have to pay a higher than average proportion of their incomes in rent. Furthermore, about 20 per cent of families are significantly poorer than the average. Therefore, in large crowded towns where there is a shortage of accommodation these families have to pay in a free market very high rents relative to their incomes.

We are, however, concerned here with the general principles upon which rents are fixed and not the wider social questions which arise when the rents paid by poor families are too high relative to their incomes. The economic problem is the conversion of rents set in the manner described above into one capital sum of money. If there is a certain plot of land which pays an annual rental of £20 a year and the law is such that the rent can never be altered, a man buying the land as an investment will consider the land as an asset that yields an annual income of £20 a year. If there is no organized capital market, as in the sixteenth century, it is impossible to predict the amount which will be given for a £20 annual income. It may be any amount ranging from about £100 to £600 and the figure finally agreed will depend upon the bargaining capacities of the buyer and seller.

If the price agreed by the buyer and seller was £400, it could either be said that the land was worth £400 or that a £20 annual income was worth £400. If the purchaser intended to occupy the land himself, he is likely to say that the land cost £400 whereas the original landlord may say that he sold his rents for £400. Once a capital market is developed, the price of an annual income from capital is known and hence the price of land which yields a fixed rent income. Thus if both buyers and sellers of land know that government bonds which pay £5 a year can be bought for £100, buyers of land cannot hope to persuade landlords to part with a £20 rental income for much less than £400. Landlords in their turn know that they cannot expect to obtain much more than £400 from the buyer of the land.

During much of the seventeenth and eighteenth centuries, the buying and selling of land was very closely associated with the buying and selling of rents. Land was one of the very few safe investments, and because the property laws impeded freehold sales of land almost all land yielded a rent to someone. As the capital market became more firmly established, the rate of interest which was thrown up by that market became widely accepted as the factor determining the capital price of land.

In the previous example of land yielding a rent of £20, a capital sum of £400 was stated to be the price if the rate of interest was 5 per cent. If the interest rate had been 10 per cent the price of £20 would be £200, but if the interest rate fell to $2\frac{1}{2}$ per cent the price of a £20 rental income would rise to £800. The relationship between interest rates and rents is customarily expressed by the phrase 'X number of years purchase'. Twenty years' purchase is equivalent to a 5 per cent return, ten years' purchase to a 10 per cent return and so on.

During the sixteenth and seventeenth centuries, rates of interest were high and the rate applied to lease purchase was 10 or even 11 per cent. During the eighteenth and nineteenth centuries, the rate fell to about 8 per cent for weekly rented property and about 4 or 5 per cent for agricultural land and building leases. During the last fifty years, taxation has introduced a very considerable complication into these calculations. The 'market' rate of interest appropriate to land purchase is the long-term rate of interest, but if this rate is equal to 6 per cent it cannot be applied directly to the rental value but must first be adjusted for the tax element. As owner-occupiers do not pay tax on the rental value of their houses they will tend to pay a higher purchase price for land than a person who intends to buy land and build houses to let. Landlords (including housing associations)[1] therefore have difficulty in obtaining land in districts where owner-occupation is very widespread. Under our existing tax arrangements an owner-occupier can always afford to pay a higher capital sum for his house than can a landlord who intends to let to a tenant with the same income as the potential owner-occupier. Thus when these two compete for land in the open market the owner-occupiers normally bid the highest price.

There is finally the complication (already mentioned at the beginning of this chapter) which only arises during periods of inflation. If the market rate of interest is applied to expected future rent levels, the purchase price of land may have no relevance whatever to the present capacity of potential occupiers to rent or to purchase through a twenty-five-year mortgage. When this situation arises, the only economic method of bringing down the price of land is by raising the rate of interest, thus simultaneously making it more expensive to hold land off the market and lowering the number of years' purchase of land.

These factors reduce the clarity with which observers can see the relationship between the price of land and its rental value. Nonetheless the relationship does exist, and one of the main objectives of this book is to show the way in which twentieth-century institutions and landlords have developed under the impact of low interest rates (compared with those of earlier centuries) and an almost complete legal freedom to buy and sell land freehold. Some of the economic opportunities which this greater freedom has created have been met by one part of the capital market and some by another. The economic benefits of specialization are as operative in the collection of capital and its investment as any other field. Gradually certain financial institutions have developed to meet the special needs of certain types of investor. As one institution becomes of predominate importance, other institutions tend to withdraw voluntarily from the field or to be pushed out by competition from the specialist institution.

In the nineteenth century there was a close partnership between

1. The position of housing associations before the Finance Act 1965.

landlords and lenders of capital. In the rather primitive state of the capital market the family solicitor occupied a position of great importance and was very often the intermediary who brought together a lender and a borrower. As the collection of capital by a relatively few large institutions progressed, the work of bringing together borrowers and lenders became less difficult and borrowers went directly to large-scale lenders.

As the large lenders became more efficient, more of the smaller lenders started to lend their money directly to the larger institutional lenders so that momentum, once attained, was continued and consolidated. At the same time, borrowers of small amounts of money became less interested in the intermediaries which lay between them and the main sources of capital. The small nineteenth-century landlord was in effect such an intermediary. He was the first beneficiary of the legal changes which permitted the older large-scale landlords to sell long leases. He was the man who brought together the owner of land (the freeholder) and the owner of capital (the mortgagee) and the occupier of land (the tenant). The small landlord of a building lease drew together the assets and needs of the other three participants in the economic venture and he received the lion's share of any profits which could be obtained.

A summary of the economic position of nineteenth-century landlords is given below.:

*Capital structure of nineteenth-century housing market*

*Freeholder*: As owner of the land he granted a ninety-nine-year building lease to the leaseholder. He retained land as a 'capital asset' which yielded 'ground rents'.

*Mortgagee*: As owner of capital he lent money to the leaseholder to cover 66 per cent of the cost of buying the lease and building a house.

*Leaseholder*: As owner of a relatively small amount of capital – 33 per cent of cost of house – he invested his money and made an income by managing the property.

*Tenant*: As a man with no capital (but an annual income) and a need to occupy a house he paid a rent in return for both the capital sunk in the house and the management undertaken by the leaseholder.

Because the capital market was not very well organized there were sometimes quite a large number of landlords and tenants. The 'tenant' above might, for instance, have a twenty-one-year lease from his landlord. The twenty-one-year leaseholder might then grant a twenty-year lease to someone else, who might in his turn let the house to a family on a weekly-tenancy agreement.

Arrangements of this kind were often made in order to spread the capital costs among as many people as possible. Each 'landlord' put some capital into the house and each tenant paid to his landlord a rent which covered the capital sunk in the house by all the investors who ranked above him. The relative inefficiency of the system can perhaps be imagined by examining the following figures:

| | |
|---|---:|
| Total cost of house and land | £1,000 |
| Value of the freeholder's land | £100 |
| Value of the 1st leaseholder's interest | £300 |
| Value of the 2nd leaseholder's interest | £200 |
| Value of the 3rd leaseholder's interest | £200 |
| Value of the 4th leaseholder's interest | £150 |
| Value of the 5th leaseholder's interest | £50 |
| Value of the occupier's interest | Nil |
| Total value of the house | £1,000 |
| Mortgagee's interest in the house (lent to first leaseholder) | £200 |
| A second mortgagee's interest in the house (lent to fourth leaseholder) | £100 |

Although this is an imaginary example, the permutations of the lending arrangements on property were almost unlimited and gave rise to considerable difficulties. In addition to the legal disputes which such a complicated chain of financial interest produced, the system was also rather 'uneconomic' as the occupier of the premises had to pay a rent which covered the costs of everyone with an interest in the property. In the nineteenth century there was little alternative to this system because very few people or institutions had sufficient capital to cover all the costs which were involved.

The development at the end of the nineteenth century and the beginning of the twentieth century of a relatively few large financial institutions made it possible for one leaseholder to carry all the capital costs. From this economic possibility it was relatively easy to cut out the leaseholder altogether and for the mortgagee and the occupier to negotiate directly without the aid of any intermediary. In 1925 the removal of the last legal constraints upon the sale of inherited real estate made it legally possible for many more freeholders to sell their land 'freehold', and thus mortgagees and the occupiers of land were given legal freedom to make whatever financial arrangement they wished. It is only in this century that it has been legally possible for millions of individuals to own a small area of freehold land.

The sale and purchase of property has become in the last forty years a matter for financial experts. The law no longer imposes constraints upon who shall and shall not own property; this aspect of land ownership is now left to market forces. The law now imposes very rigid rules on what may be built on or removed from land, but town-planning and public-health laws make no attempt to direct or retain capital in land and houses. Today we see the full effects of the economic developments which lay behind the Act of 1572; any man with sufficient resources can now purchase land under any arrangement which is financially viable. Viability is judged by reference to what a lender is willing to do. We still, however, speak of 'landlords' and refer to them as if they were some identifiable social group.

A modern property company however, has much more in common with an institution which lends money, like a bank or an insurance company, than with the old type of landlord. The difference lies in the fact that a modern property company is continually aware of the capital value of its assets. If it were not for certain aspects of the tax laws, such companies would as soon buy and sell property as rent it out.

In the nineteenth century the state of the conveyancing laws would by themselves have been a great discouragement to too frequent sales of real estate. For this reason, among many others, it is most unlikely that large property companies could have flourished before the law of real property was reformed.

# CHAPTER 3

# Loans and their Economic Results

There are four types of loan which have been used to finance house ownership. Each type of loan has different economic consequences and risks for the borrower as well as different advantages and disadvantages for the lender. We shall first consider the four types of loan, then some of their economic consequences:

1. The loan which has to be repaid in full on a stated day.
2. The loan which is only repaid when the lender asks for repayment.
3. The loan which is never repaid, or only repaid when the borrower wishes to make repayment.
4. The loan which is repaid by instalments.

### 1. Loans repaid in full on a stated day

The first type of loan is of very ancient origin and is not very convenient for those who wish to buy a house unless the date of repayment is ten or twenty years after the borrowing date. It is a type of loan particularly favoured by the trader or manufacturer who expects to make a sufficient profit in the foreseeable future to enable him to repay the loan on the stated day. It is also a convenient form of loan for a builder who intends to sell houses, not to keep them.

### 2. Loans repaid when the lender asks for repayment

The second type of loan is only useful to the house purchaser if there are a lot of people willing to lend on this basis. If a mortgage can be called in on three to six months' notice, borrowers may be very greatly inconvenienced unless there are a large number of people willing to lend on this basis so that a new mortgage can be negotiated during the period of notice which is given before a mortgage is withdrawn. This is the type of mortgage loan which was most common in the nineteenth century. Mortgages were seldom for a fixed term of years, and most of the money lent was controlled by the trustees of charities, widows and orphans. As such trustee funds were relatively plentiful, the risks of having one mortgage called in when another could not be raised appear to have been regarded as negligible.

Provided that funds are sufficiently plentiful, this type of loan is almost ideal for the small property owner. During the term of the loan, only interest has to be paid; there is no repayment of principal. The outgoings of the owner are therefore kept to a minimum. If the owner wishes to take action to avoid the risks of not being able to raise another mortgage when the existing one is called in, he can save and accumulate a 'sinking-fund'. This fund will be under his own control and can fluctuate in accordance with his personal assessment of the risks of not getting another mortgage. Furthermore, any interest earned on the sinking-fund is his.

### 3. *Loans repaid when the borrower decides to repay*

The third type of loan, which may never be repaid, is the 'ideal' type of loan for the property owner. Loans of this type were made in the nineteenth century to corporate bodies but not to individuals. Probably the most famous of such loans are the British Government Consols, but less important corporate bodies of the nineteenth century could borrow on the condition that the loan need not be repaid until the borrower chose to make repayment. The London County Council 1920 stock is an example. Another type of financial arrangement which has much in common with the 'never repaid' loan is the ordinary stock of a joint stock company. The 'ordinary' share investor in such a company has no right to demand the return of his money from the company until the firm is liquidated and all assets returned to the shareholders. This arrangement introduces into the financial affairs of such companies an important element of flexibility. Dwelling-houses have, however, never been extensively financed by arrangements which do not involve the repayment of capital borrowed.

In the last century, corporate bodies such as local authorities arranged their finances in the confident expectation that, so long as they paid the interest on their loans, they would not have any difficulty in obtaining a new loan to replace any which might be called in. The proper amortization of a loan is an 'invention' made in the nineteenth century, and we tend nowadays to forget that a considerable knowledge of arithmetic is needed in the proper management and balancing of a sinking-fund. It was not until the end of the nineteenth century that the Local Government Board successfully imposed on local authorities definite loan terms and the creation of precisely calculated sinking-funds for the repayment of loans.

A sinking-fund makes provision for the repayment of a loan by setting apart a fixed annual sum to be invested. Through these payments and the accumulation of compound interest, the sinking-fund grows each year and comes to equal the loan debt when this is due for repayment. During the nineteenth century some local-authority officials appear to have thought of a 'sinking-fund' as a special fund set up to meet any deficit which might arise when a project was completed.

The Lord Provost of Glasgow, in giving evidence to the Select Committee on the Repayment of Loans by Local Authorities in 1902, said that the loan of £1,250,000 borrowed by Glasgow under the Glasgow Improvement Act 1866 was still outstanding, and he saw no reason why a sinking-fund should be set up to arrange for its repayment. As the buildings erected under the Act were of great value, when the loan term expired 'posterity' could repay the loan out of income and other resources, or sell the assets which had been created, or raise a new loan to pay off the old one. If any of these actions did not raise sufficient monies to repay the loan, then a deficit would be recorded and a 'sinking-fund' set up to meet this deficit.

This is not, however, the modern meaning of the term 'sinking-fund', which relates to a regular annual payment of monies into a special account and the accumulation of all interest earned on the annual instalments. The sinking-funds of local authorities have now attained a rigidity and even a sanctity which was unknown in the nineteenth century. In Plymouth, when a hotel and theatre were built before 1835, no provision was made for the repayment of the £30,000 loan raised for this project. In 1902 the property was re-let on a ninety-nine-year lease at a rental of £4,800 and a condition that £10,000 was spent on improving the buildings. This meant that the property in 1902 was worth about £130,000, and the Town Clerk of Plymouth seems to have regarded either a sinking-fund or the repayment of the original loan as an unnecessary financial arrangement imposed upon Plymouth by the Local Government Board.[1]

## 4. *Loans repaid by annual instalments of principal and interest*

The fourth type of loan, which is repaid by annual instalments of principal, was available to the private house purchaser in the nineteenth century from a building society. The first building societies worked on the simplest principles of arithmetic. Several men formed one society

1. See 'Evidence Taken Before Select Committee on the Repayment of Loans by Local Authorities', British Parliamentary Papers, vol. VIII, 1902.

and each member paid a regular weekly sum to the society funds. When the funds were large enough, one house was bought and allotted to one of the members. This member repaid the money he had borrowed from the society as quickly as he could, and in the meantime all other members continued to make their regular weekly subscriptions. As soon as possible, a second house was bought, until eventually every member had a house. However, the regular payment of subscriptions was a great burden on the members and many failed to maintain their payments in times of sickness and unemployment. Sometimes a man would have to wait ten years or more before his turn to get a house was reached, and many despaired and left the society, forfeiting their right to a house.

These early building societies were a part of the general movement among working men for self help, but they had little chance of success while all the members of any one society wanted a house. For the societies to become sound financial institutions, they needed some members who would only be lenders; such members would add to the pool of funds available but not, at the same time, add to the demands made upon those funds. In the first half of the century some societies developed along these lines, and in 1846 this development had reached the point where a permanent building society could be formed. As soon as the lenders were no longer identical with those wishing to borrow money, there was no reason for the termination of the society when the last member had a house. Instead, as one group of borrowers repaid their loans, another group could be given mortgages, the lenders remaining the same throughout. During the second half of the nineteenth century the societies became, in effect, 'banks'. Capital was lent to them on short notice and lent out by them on five- to fifteen-year mortgages.

Theoretically, a 'permanent' building society is a perfectly sound financial institution, and they normally operate in the traditions of the most orthodox banks. The men who started and organized these early societies were, on the whole, men of extreme honesty and caution, and they were content to operate in one district and confine their activities to meeting the needs of small shopkeepers, clerks and other fairly poor savers and house purchasers. However, a few societies were involved in minor speculative activity and occasionally the untrained and ill-paid secretaries of the societies fraudulently converted some of the funds to their own use. However, these activities were of less importance in slowing down the rate of growth of the movement than the profound ignorance of book-keeping and the banking risks of over-lending which characterized many of the officers employed. Most of the officers were unpaid or even voluntary workers and attended to their society's business at a few evening meetings each month.[1]

In these circumstances the accumulation of savings by relatively poor people was a very slow process. It was not until 1874 that the foundations for a really rapid expansion were laid by the Building Societies Act 1874, which gave the societies unambiguous statutory powers to borrow. Before this date some of the societies had borrowed from banks and other large-scale lenders, but the legality of such borrowing was doubtful and many societies had resisted the temptation to increase their funds by such means. The right to borrow was of great importance, since it freed the societies from dependence upon the small saver. The right was nominally curbed by Section 15 of the Act which prohibited borrowing in excess of two thirds of the amount for the time being secured by mortgages from members. This, however, only meant that the societies could borrow as much money as they could lend out on mortgage while preventing them from borrowing for other purposes.

By 1890 the societies had between them over £48 million lent out on mortgages, and this mode of financing house purchase seemed to be well established when the speculative activities of a prominent Member of Parliament, who controlled the funds of the Liberator Building Society, led to the bankruptcy of that society and the rapid withdrawal of funds from other societies. Public alarm was somewhat allayed by the Building Societies Act of 1894, which strengthened the control exercised by the Chief Registrar of Friendly Societies, but between 1894 and 1911 membership of the societies did not increase very much, although the members which they retained gradually increased their investments. The money lent on mortgages grew from a low level of £38 million in 1894 to almost £60 million in 1911.

Another serious bankruptcy in 1911 (the Birbeck) did not rock the movement as the Liberator crash had done in the 1890s. Most of the societies had by then become individually sufficiently strong to withstand the immediate panic which follows the failure of any large financial institution. From 1911 through to 1919 the societies consolidated their position and built up a reputation for probity and good solid business sense. Although the amount lent on mortgage fell substantially during the war years, the level of their membership was maintained. In 1919 they at last managed not only to equal but to exceed the membership of 1890. The fall in mortgages during the war

1. See Annual Reports of Chief Registrar of Friendly Societies for the Registrar's complaints about the lack of book-keeping knowledge.

was entirely due to a loss of demand for mortgages and was not accompanied by any loss of funds.

In the years 1919 to 1939 the total funds invested in mortgaged property rose every year at an average rate of 13·2 per cent a year, the years of most rapid growth being 1924 and 1925[1] and those of slowest growth 1932 and 1939. The most significant statistic of building societies is the amount which they advance each year on new mortgages. In 1913 it was about £9 million, in 1919 £15·8 million, and in 1920 there was a further increase to £25 million. These high amounts were largely due to the withdrawal of funds from short-term wartime investments, and in 1921 the amount lent on new mortgages fell back to £19·7 million. However, the societies' membership continued to rise and in 1923 the amount lent exceeded the 1920 level. It was not until 1932 that there was again a brief halt to the annual increase in the amount lent out each year on new mortgages. In 1931 the amount lent was £90 million and in 1932 this fell back to £82 million. Although the general economic depression continued into 1933, the societies were able to maintain their momentum and lent over £103 million during the year. The inter-war peak was reached in 1936 when £140 million was lent.

During the Second World War the societies behaved much as they had during 1914–18. Mortgages were repaid, and since the demand for new mortgages was low, funds were invested in government stock. In 1945 the building societies again faced a situation of acute housing shortage and the annual amount advanced on mortgages rose rapidly to £188 million. However, since 1945 the progress of the building societies has been rather less spectacular than it was in the inter-war period. From 1949 to the end of 1952 the level of the societies' new mortgage advances remained fairly constant. Then from 1952 to 1955 they rose rapidly from £266 million a year to £394 million. In the three years 1956 through to 1958 the amount fell a little and then steadied at about £370 million. In 1959 the Government gave a boost to the societies by making £100 million available to them under the special conditions of the House Purchase and Housing Act 1959; this government assistance coincided with an increase in the funds available from the general public, with the result that in 1959 and 1960 advances reached a new peak of £517 million and £560 million respectively. By 1963 the amount had increased further to £849 million.

From 1946 to the end of 1963, the average annual growth of the

1. See Chapter 6, pages 84–5, for the 1923 Act providing subsidies to local-authority and private-enterprise housing. The growth of the building societies in 1924 and 1925 may have been a coincidence or it may have owed something to the 1923 Act.

3

societies' outstanding mortgage balances has been 10·6 per cent compared with the pre-war average of 13·2 per cent. As the post-war period has been one of rising costs and prices, whereas the inter-war period was one of deflation and falling price-levels, the societies have lost more of their drive and rate of expansion than the crude statistics suggest. Nevertheless, their total progress since 1900 has been impressive and they have played a crucial role in the development of the English and Welsh housing markets. Today approximately 20 per cent of all families are living in a house which they have already bought and a further 20 per cent are living in houses which they are buying. Local authorities and insurance companies have contributed to this situation, but the financial achievement which has enabled over 40 per cent of all families to live in their own house is largely due to the building-society movement.

*Economic effects of a loan repaid by annual instalments of principal*

It is now necessary to consider the economic consequences of the amortization of a loan through a building-society type of mortgage. It will be remembered that the loan which was never repaid was termed the 'ideal' loan for a property owner because the annual outgoings were kept to a minimum. The owner who can obtain such a mortgage possesses the full equity interests in the property in exactly the same way

*Table 1: Showing annual outgoings on a loan of £1,000.*

| Year | Building society loan | | | No repayment of capital loan |
| | Annual payments | Capital | Interest | Interest |
| --- | --- | --- | --- | --- |
| | £ | £ | £ | £ |
| 1 | 129·5 | 79·5 | 50·0 | 50 |
| 2 | 129·5 | 83·5 | 46·0 | 50 |
| 3 | 129·5 | 87·6 | 41·9 | 50 |
| 4 | 129·5 | 92·0 | 37·5 | 50 |
| 5 | 129·5 | 96·6 | 32·9 | 50 |
| 6 | 129·5 | 101·5 | 28·0 | 50 |
| 7 | 129·5 | 106·5 | 23·0 | 50 |
| 8 | 129·5 | 111·9 | 17·6 | 50 |
| 9 | 129·5 | 117·5 | 12·0 | 50 |
| 10 | 129·5 | 123·3 | 6·2 | 50 |
| Totals | | £1,000·0 | £295·1 | £500 |

as the owner of a house mortgaged to a building society. There is, however, a highly significant economic difference between the two types of loan. The building-society loan is so arranged that the family pays most for the house when the family income is highest and least for the house in old age when income is at its lowest. This occurs because mortgages are usually arranged so that all repayments are made before the age of retirement. However, to obtain this considerable benefit the outgoings on the house during the working period of the family are usually so high that (except in inflationary periods) the house can seldom be let at a profit. This can be shown by a simple example in Table 1, which shows the mortgage rate of interest as 5 per cent and the amount borrowed as £1,000 over a ten-year period from a building society. The annual repayments of interest and capital will then be £129·5.

In this example the owner who obtained a loan from a building society pays £1,295 over the ten-year period of purchase. An owner who obtains a mortgage upon which only interest is paid, pays out £500 during the ten-year period and still owes £1,000 at the end of that period. If this owner has to repay the £1,000 at the end of the tenth year his total outgoings will be £1,500, but if he can obtain a new mortgage or retain the existing one his outgoings will be much smaller than those incurred by a borrower from a building society.

The possibility of obtaining another mortgage depends upon the condition of the house and the demand for such houses. If the house was new at the beginning of the ten-year period, it is very probable that a new mortgage can be obtained as long as lenders have funds available. A ten-year-old house is almost as good a house as a new one, and in the nineteenth century funds were fairly readily available and new mortgages often obtained. As the life-span of the owner of a house is usually much shorter than the life of the house (assuming that a man buys a house when he is about thirty years old) there is no economic reason why a man should ever have to repay the mortgage so long as lenders exist who will give mortgages on dwellings which have an expected future life of thirty or more years.[1] Thus in looking at this example the reader should bear in mind that in the nineteenth century there were lenders willing to keep their money permanently out on mortgage; it should also be borne in mind that although it may be 'moral' to repay a loan eventually, there is no special economic virtue in repaying one if it is not legally or financially necessary to do so.

1. The increased 'expectation of life' of both borrowers and lenders gives both parties to a loan an increased incentive to repay loans.

If the owner of the house wished to let it, how much rent could he expect to get? It is impossible to give any definite figure. The poorer a family is relative to other families, the higher is likely to be the percentage of family income which is devoted to rent and food. As the family income approximates to the average income of all families, the proportion spent on rent tends to fall. Since the nineteenth century there has been a tendency to think that a rent is 'high' if it exceeds 30 per cent of income and 'low' if it is less than 15 per cent. However, ideas about 'high' and 'low' rents only have meaning in relation to some customary rent level. If nearly all families paid 10 per cent of their income in rent then the few families who paid 15 per cent of their income in rent would regard their rents as 'high'; but those same families would regard their rent as 'low' if all other families were paying 30 per cent of their income in rent. At present many people seem to think that a 'reasonable' rent is one that does not exceed 20 to 25 per cent of a tenant's income. This opinion is sufficiently widely held for prospective landlords to calculate the profits they might obtain by letting houses on the assumption that they can obtain a gross rent equal to about 25 per cent of their tenant's income.

If this convention is accepted it should immediately be clear from the example given above that the owner who has a mortgage from a building society is in a much less favourable position than the other owner. If the whole capital sunk in the house (£1,500) is to pay a return of 5 per cent the total interest payments will be £75. If the income of a potential occupier is £500 per annum (see Chapter 9 for a discussion of house prices and annual income levels), the house can probably be let at a rent of £100 to £150 per annum. The landlord who does not have to repay any of the principal would have £25 per annum to cover the costs of management, repairs and voids if he let the house at £100, and he would have £75 to cover these expenses if he let at £150. The £150 rent would more than cover the landlord's costs—it would give him a bigger return on his share of the capital of £500 than 5 per cent and is an economically viable proposition.

The owner who has borrowed from a building society is in a very inferior position. A rent of £100 will not cover the annual outgoings to the society (£129·5), and even if the house was let at £150 a year it is still not a viable proposition. The owner would only obtain £20·5 for the return on his own capital of £500 and there is nothing left over to to cover the expenses of management.

At the end of the ten-year loan period the landlord who has no mortgage on his house is undoubtedly in a much better financial position than the one who still has a mortgage. But ten years is a very long time to wait for a return on invested capital. If the loan period is lengthened to twenty years, the capital and interest payments to a building society fall to £80 a year. At a rental of £100 a year this will give the owner of the house a return of only 4 per cent on his capital with nothing over for management expenses. A rent of £150 certainly gives an adequate return, but it represents 30 per cent of the income of the family for whom we assumed the house was suitable. In view of these calculations, it is hardly surprising that few investors use building societies to finance houses which they wish to let.

We do know, however, that many of the mortgages granted by building societies in the nineteenth century were to small shopkeepers who bought one or two houses as an investment. This financial operation was only profitable because most of the society mortgages were on leasehold property. This meant that the ground landlord 'lent' some of his capital on a non-repayable basis to the leaseholder.[1]

If we re-work the example given on page 30, assuming the existence of a ground landlord who charges a ground rent of £18·75 (the free-holder values the land at £375 and gets 5 per cent on this sum as a 'ground rent') and a leasehold price for the house of £1,125, the purchaser of the lease would probably be able to obtain a mortgage of £750, leaving a balance of £375 to be invested by the leaseholder. A ten-year mortgage at 5 per cent would require annual payments of interest and capital equalling approximately £97. A 5 per cent return on the owner's own capital would be £18·75. Therefore the total annual outgoings would be £134·5 compared with the total in the first example of £154·5 (£129·5 plus £25 interest on the owner's own capital). This is not a very large difference, but with a fifteen- to twenty-year mortgage it would be possible to make a profit by letting the house at a net rent of £100 or £120 a year.

Table 2 shows the relationship between (1) the rate of interest, (2) the length of the loan, and (3) the percentage of income required to repay a loan which *exactly* equals the annual income of the borrower. The table should be read in the following way. Assume any annual income, say for example £500. Then if it is assumed that a man borrows exactly £500 from a building society, the table can be used to find out the percentage of his income which will be needed to meet annual payments which must be made to the building society. If the interest rate charged by the society is 5 per cent and the term of mortgage

1. Seymour J. Price, *Building Societies. Their Origin and History*, Franey, 1958, p. 273.

thirty years the owner will pay 6·5 per cent of his annual income to repay the loan, and the annual interest charges; 6·5 per cent of £500 is equal to £32·5, and this is the amount in cash which the man will have to pay. If the man borrows twice as much as his annual income (£1,000), his annual repayments will be twice as large (£65 per annum) and the percentage of his income spent on 'buying' his house will be 13 per cent.

The relationships given in the table hold for all incomes, but the reader must remember that the table ties the mortgage down to the level of income. Given the level of income the loan can be expressed as a multiple of income and the table can then be used to calculate the amount of annual income needed to 'service the loan'.

An inspection of Tables 2 and 3 should convince the reader that a building-society loan is singularly ill-adapted to meet the needs of a man who wishes to buy a house to let at a profit, but a final example may make this point a little more forcibly. A man earning £2,000 in 1965 and working in London would probably have to pay at least £500 per annum for a suitable house in or near London. A man with this income is unlikely to wish to live in a tenement house and he certainly cannot afford to live in a luxury flat. He is, however, quite likely to be willing to live in a house which would sell for £6,000 or £7,000 in the suburbs.

If he bought a house for £7,000 in the suburbs through a building society and obtained a £6,000 mortgage for thirty years, he would have to pay nearly 22 per cent (£440) of his income to meet his obligations to the building society. If after buying the house he decided to let it instead of occupying it himself, he must obtain £440 plus a return on his own capital of £1,000 (say £60) making a total of £500.

To cover the costs of insurance, management and repairs falling upon the landlord, at least another £100 is required,[1] making a total net rent of £600. Thus with a building-society type of loan, £600 is the approximate annual 'supply price' of the house, but will a demand exist to match this supply price? It seems hardly likely that a demand will exist from men earning £2,000 a year for houses to let at net rents of £600. In 1965 men who earned £2,400 and could afford to pay a rent of £600 could (if they had a capital of £1,000) buy a better house costing a little over £8,000 and pay to service a £7,200 mortgage over thirty years, £528.[2] If the tax position is taken into account, the 'supply price' from a

1. See Chapter 4 on taxation of landlords and calculation of the amount of tax which would have to be paid on the whole of the rent.
2. See Chapter 5 on taxation of individuals to obtain net cost of loan to borrower.

*Table 2: Table for the calculation of the percentage of income spent on the repayment of capital plus interest on a building-society loan which is exactly equal to the annual income of the borrower.*

| Rate of interest % | Percentage of income spent on mortgage payments over a term of: | | | |
|---|---|---|---|---|
| | 10 years | 20 years | 30 years | 40 years |
| 4 | 12·32 | 7·36 | 5·8 | 5·04 |
| 4½ | 12·64 | 7·69 | 6·12 | 5·45 |
| 5 | 12·95 | 8·0 | 6·5 | 5·85 |
| 5½ | 13·25 | 8·36 | 6·87 | 6·21 |
| 6 | 13·56 | 8·7 | 7·26 | 6·66 |
| 6½ | 13·91 | 9·1 | 7·67 | 7·08 |

*Table 3: Building-society mortgage rate. This gives the interest rates charged by most building societies over the period 1920 to 1963.*

| Year | Mortgage rate % |
|---|---|
| 1920 | 6½ |
| 1921–32 | 6 |
| 1933 | 5½ |
| 1934–5 | 5 |
| 1936–9 | 4½ |
| 1940 | 5 |
| 1941 | 5½ |
| 1942–3 | 5 |
| 1944–5 | 4½ |
| 1946–52 | 4 |
| 1953–5 | 4½ |
| 1956 | 5½ |
| 1957–9 | 6 |
| 1960 | 5½ |
| 1961 | 6 |
| 1962 | 6½ |
| 1963 | 6 |
| 1964 | 6¾ |

building society for a better house is less than the 'supply price' from a private landlord for the inferior house.

The examples given in this chapter have shown that a landlord cannot profitably use a building-society loan if he wishes to let property and that it is normally to the occupier's advantage to use the facilities of a building society rather than the services of a landlord. This does not depend upon the fact that, if you can afford to buy something, it may be better to do so than to hire it; the argument does not rely on any assumptions about the relative desirability of buying or renting. The competitive position of the building societies *versus* the landlord rest entirely upon the economic fact that the societies have quite intentionally made their loan terms competitive with those of landlords. A building society sets the terms of its loans in relation to what it thinks the occupier can *afford* to pay. Interest rates are beyond the control of the societies, but the term of the loan is not and when interest rates rise the societies lengthen the term of the loan. They thereby ensure that borrowers will continue to find the societies' terms and conditions acceptable.

The societies have been in operation (in their modern form) for almost 120 years and have effectively ousted the private landlord from the middle-income residential property market. The only reason why the societies have not utterly routed the private landlord from all sectors of the market is their refusal to give 100 per cent mortgages, which effectively debars a great many families from owner-occupation. While, however, the capital market has produced the financial institution we know as 'building societies', the market has produced no comparable institution which meets the needs of small landlords. The small landlord can only borrow today from his bank or a building society. There is no specialist institution to meet his needs, and as banks do not usually give long-term loans and the building societies are unsuitable, landlords are 'deprived' of capital. It is not the rates of interest which the landlord is unable to meet, but the insistence of twentieth-century lenders on the return of their money. Today if a lender is willing to lend on a non-repayable basis he insists that his asset should be 'marketable'. A lender will lend to 'A' if the legal document relating to the loan can be sold with ease to 'B'. Government bonds and public company shares can be sold easily and therefore lenders are willing to lend to the Government or, for instance, to large firms such as Woolworth's or I.C.I., but loans to an individual cannot be sold in this way and today very few willing lenders could be found to lend to an individual who was not going to repay the loan in the foreseeable future (say two to five years).

*Reasons for the decline of the private mortgagee*

So far an attempt has been made to show why a building-society loan is not suitable for an investor who wishes to let a house which costs several times the annual income of the prospective tenant. It is now necessary to consider why a building society offers a more secure investment for the person with capital to lend than the older type of mortgage. Mortgages of the nineteenth century, which could be called in on three to six months' notice, gave the mortgagee a fairly safe investment. So long as the house had been properly surveyed before the mortgage was granted the mortgagee was not likely to lose his capital. He could, however, never be quite certain that the mortgagor would be able to repay the capital within the period of notice. As a last resort the mortgagee could foreclose and sell the property, but such actions are very troublesome and any hurried sale of property tends to lower the selling-price. Because of these difficulties a private mortgage is a very 'illiquid' form of investment.

The building societies are able to give their investors a much higher degree of liquidity by working on the banking principle of always keeping sufficient cash in hand to meet the demands made upon them by their share investors and depositors. The societies' managers know from experience that if they keep about 15 per cent of all monies invested in the form of cash or highly liquid assets they will be able to meet all the requests made to them by investors who wish to withdraw their capital. As the funds invested with the societies have increased, the risks of default have lessened. However, there remains some financial risk in the acceptance of extremely large sums from single investors who may want all their capital back as soon as interest rates on other investments rise, and in the early part of the decade 1930–40 some societies refused to accept capital from investors who would certainly have withdrawn most of their money as soon as investment on the Stock Exchange or in business became profitable again.

The management expenses of a building society are not very high and the investor can therefore obtain almost as high a rate of interest by lending his money to a society as he could get if he lent it out directly himself. In 1963 investors who were liable to the standard rate of tax were obtaining a return of about 5·75 per cent *before* tax by investing in societies which paid them 3·5 or 3·75 per cent (tax paid). It must also be remembered that building societies charge the current long-term rate of interest to their borrowers, although the example on page 30 shows that some of the capital is only lent for a very short period of time. It is this constant return of the capital to the societies which gives them their stability and financial capacity to adjust to changing economic circumstances. It also makes it almost impossible for an honestly run society to go bankrupt. So long as the managers of societies keep within the law and make careful survey of all properties upon which mortgages are granted, they can hardly fail to obtain the return of all capital lent. Since the mortgage is always secured on the whole value of the house, a forced sale of the property will normally raise at least the amount required to repay to the mortgagee any capital debt outstanding from the original loan, which equalled from 66 to 90 per cent of the valuation of the property.

We have now to consider the reasons for the growth of the societies during the twenties and thirties of this century. Note has already been made of the fact that by 1914 the movement had overcome its most difficult early problems of financial instability due to speculative mis-management of funds. It was also beginning to benefit, like so many other financial institutions, from the general improvement in the level of education of its officers and in particular from the specialized education provided by such bodies as the Chartered Institute of Secretaries, which was founded in 1891.

The main reason for the growth in the immediate post-First World War period seems to stem quite simply from the fact that there was a large demand for houses and the building societies had funds accumu-lated from the war years. From 1919 to 1922 or 1923 they must have been one of the few available sources for mortgages. Most of the nineteenth-century mortgages had been made with trustee funds under the control of solicitors. These funds had a very limited number of outlets and mortgages were highly favoured by the legal profession, whose knowledge of property law far outweighed a knowledge of financial institutions and economics. However, the funds which solicitors received during the war had to be dealt with immediately; solicitors could not merely lodge the money in a bank until hostilities ceased and the demand for mortgages returned to normal. From both the legal and national point of view an excellent alternative investment for such funds existed—the enormously swollen National Debt.

Unfortunately we have no way of knowing how solicitors reacted to this situation. During the war they must have channelled some of the funds they held into British Government Stock because there was so little else that they could do with it. New mortgages could be created after the war with any current funds which they controlled, and such mortgages would presumably have paid 6 or even 6·5 per cent interest since this was the rate of interest which building societies were obtain-ing. What probably happened in the early twenties was a simple deflection of funds but by no means a complete withdrawal. However, even a small deflection of funds would have aided the building societies by reducing the competition which the private mortgagee represents to a building society.

The funds of trustees remain today an important although, in relation to other institutions, a declining source of finance for individual property owners who have sufficient personal reliability and public standing to satisfy Trustees of their credit-worthiness. In the table of estimated wealth of individuals published by the Inland Revenue for 1961, the money on mortgage of real estate was estimated to be £585 million. This was equal to 15·7 per cent of the total estimated value of the shares and deposits in building societies.

Some indication of the relative fall in investment in private mortgages is given by the Commissioners of Inland Revenue in their annual reports since 1897–8. From the tables of gross capital value of personal property subject to estate duty, it is possible to calculate the percentage of total personal property which was held in the form of 'money out on mortgage' at the time when persons paying estate duty died. For the period between 1897 and 1914 an average of 6·5 per cent of total personal property was in the form of mortgages. Between the wars the amount fell to an average of 3·3 per cent and in the period since 1950 the annual average has fallen further to 1·8 per cent. As, however, the total value of personal property has been rising since the beginning of the century the amount of money out on mortgage has not declined in absolute value.

The fall in the percentage of total personal property lent on mortgage first becomes significant in 1920–1, when 'money on mortgage' was 4·5 per cent of all personal property. The comparable figure for 1913–14 was 6·4 per cent. During the twenties and thirties the percentage declined fairly steadily and by 1937–8 it had fallen to 2·7 per cent. By 1961–2 the figure was down to 1·5 per cent. These statistics confirm the generally held opinion that the building societies have now supplanted the private mortgagee. The Trustees Investments Act of 1961, which greatly extended the powers of trustees to invest funds in profit-making concerns, can be expected to reduce further the amount of money available for private mortgage. As, however, the shares of building societies are now included in the schedule of trustee investments, some trustee funds may flow into house mortgages via the societies. In the next chapter the way in which taxation of the landlord has lagged behind these financial developments will be considered.

CHAPTER 4

# Taxation of Landlords

The taxes which are imposed upon landlords are in principle exactly the same taxes as those imposed upon any other group of taxpayers. Landlords are assessed to tax upon the current income which they derive from the ownership of land and buildings. Up to 1963 all owners of dwelling-houses were taxed under Schedule A, whether the 'income' which was derived from the house was income from rents or a real income which occupiers obtained by virtue of living in the house. In this chapter we are not concerned with the general principle of placing a tax upon dwelling-houses, but only with the legal provisions which have been made for taxing the income derived from letting houses. In Chapters 9 and 10 we shall consider more generally the question of whether taxes should be imposed upon the imputed real income which accrues to an owner-occupier of a dwelling.

Stated very simply, the present position of a landlord is that all his net income from rents is taxed under Schedule D (Case VIII); profits made from the sale of land or the sale of a lease are taxed under Case VI of Schedule D. For purposes of taxation 'net rental income' is the income which remains after the landlord has deducted all the expenses he incurs in the collection of the rents, maintenance of the property and the payment of any interest on the capital invested in the house. The position of the landlord is basically that he collects a gross rental income and deducts all his expenses and then pays tax upon any income which is left. The levels of tax are determined by the level of net income in exactly the same way as for any other person or company paying income tax, surtax or profits tax.

However, if the financial position of landlords is examined in closer detail, it is found that they have to pay tax upon the capital which is invested in the property.

The effect of the present taxes levied upon the revenue obtained from residential property can be seen most clearly by examining the taxes which fall on rent derived from improvements made to Victorian houses. These houses are now seventy to a hundred years old and cannot be expected to last for more than another fifteen to thirty years. The installation of a bathroom is, however, commercially worthwhile if the capital spent can earn the current rate of return and the asset is depreciated so that the capital invested is returned to the owner by the time the house has to be demolished.

The return of the capital can be arranged through a sinking-fund, which is accumulated each year by putting aside some of the rent revenue. The monies invested in the sinking-fund can earn interest (at about 3 per cent net of tax), and as the interest earned can also be accumulated the annual amount needed for the sinking-fund will be less than the actual amount of capital spent. For instance, if £100 was spent on a house with a life of fifteen years, £5 7s. 6d. would be needed for the sinking-fund each year if the interest earned on this money was 3 per cent net of tax. The capital instalments put into the sinking-fund would amount to £80 12s. 6d. over a fifteen-year period and the accumulated interest would amount to a further £19 7s. 6d., making a total of £100. When a landlord is deciding whether or not he will improve a dwelling with a life of fifteen years, he will take into consideration the amount he needs for a sinking-fund as well as the return he will obtain on his capital.

Under the rent-controlling legislation landlords were permitted a gross 8 per cent on capital spent on improvements until the rate was raised by the Housing Act 1961 to 12½ per cent. However, these are 'gross' rates of return and no allowance was made in the Act for a sinking-fund. The sinking-fund has therefore to be obtained from the gross return. The profitability of improving a house with a life of fifteen years has therefore to be measured in the following way:

| | | | |
|---|---|---|---|
| Annual sinking-fund instalment | £5 | 7s. | 6d. |
| Annual tax payable on £12 10s. | £6 | 14s. | 4d. |
| Total outgoings | £12 | 1s. | 10d. |
| Total rent revenue | £12 | 10s. | 0d. |
| Total 'net' profit for landlord on expenditure of £100 | | 8s. | 2d. |

The profit of 8s. 2d. is all that is left for the landlord after he has paid tax at 10s. 9d. (the company rate of tax) and put aside the money for the sinking-fund. If the Inland Revenue permitted the landlord to depreciate his property over the fifteen-year period, the profit to the landlord would be £3 3s. 3d. after payment of tax, instead of 8s. 2d. Table 4 (page 42) shows the return which a landlord makes on £100 spent in improving a house with a life of fifteen to thirty years when the gross return on capital is 12½ per cent. The 'net' return on capital has been given before the payment of income or profits tax on that part of the revenue which is not needed for the sinking-fund. The figures given can therefore be compared directly with the investment earnings on other types of investment. The income-tax payment of 7s. 9d. is the tax rate appropriate to many individual landlords and small housing associations or property companies. The higher tax rate of 10s. 9d. is paid by larger housing associations or property companies which have an annual income exceeding £15,000.

*Table 4: Summary of tax position.*

| Expected life of house in years | 'Net' rate of return on capital when gross return is 12½% | |
|---|---|---|
| | *Tax at 7s. 9d.* | *Tax at 10s. 9d.* |
| 15 | 3·729% | 0·871% |
| 20 | 6·425% | 4·454% |
| 25 | 8·021% | 6·571% |
| 30 | 9·067% | 7·954% |

As money cannot at present be borrowed at less than about 6½ per cent interest, it is clear that landlords who are borrowing money from outside sources cannot 'afford' to improve their property unless it has a life of about thirty years. If depreciation allowances were given to owners who let residential property it would be commercially worth improving houses with a life of twenty years. In passing it is perhaps worth noting that while landlords obtain little benefit from a 12½ per cent gross return, the tenants have the burden of paying this high gross return on capital spent on their dwellings. The old gross return of 8 per cent was raised because the lack of arrangements for depreciating assets made it uneconomic for landlords to improve houses with a life of less than thirty-five to forty years with an 8 per cent gross return. However, even a 12½ per cent gross return is insufficient to induce most landlords paying tax at 10s. 9d. in the pound, and borrowing at current rates of interest, to undertake improvements.

Readers who are unaccustomed to modern methods of finance and the organization of precisely calculated sinking-funds may be a little bewildered by the references to 'gross' and 'net' returns on investments. However, there is nothing very complex about these arrangements, which are designed to enable the investor to get his money back. Just as a man who invests money in the Post Office Savings Bank expects to get an annual interest payment on his money and the return of his capital when he wants it, so a landlord will not invest money unless he can get the capital back and the current annual return on that capital. For the past 160 years, however, the tax laws of the United Kingdom have taken no account of the fact that a dwelling has only a limited life. Taxes on residential property are imposed on the assumption that dwellings last for ever and that sinking-funds are a luxury which some landlords like to have and some do not. The annual payments into the fund are not regarded as a necessity and are not, therefore, classified for tax purposes as a 'cost'.

The relatively unfavourable tax position of the landlord was not created intentionally by the legislature, but the landlord's position has been allowed to grow relatively worse with each succeeding decade of tax history. This may be because the position of manufacturers or individual owner-occupiers seems more easily to attract the attention of Members of Parliament and to obtain remedial action from governments. The complaints of landlords are certainly heard, but for the past fifty years have been thought to relate to the baleful effects of rent control rather than to the prolonged impact of an antiquated tax belief in the 'immortality' of a dwelling-house. For this reason it is worth looking very briefly at the history of income taxation.

In concentrating upon income tax, the impact of local rates should not be entirely forgotten. There is, however, quite an extensive literature on the burden of rates and they will not therefore be discussed here. It should, however, be remembered that 'rates' are an indirect tax imposed upon dwelling-houses. If a flat is let at an inclusive rent of £3 per week (£2 rent, £1 rates), the flat has an indirect tax of 50 per cent imposed upon it. The imposition of this tax must necessarily reduce the amount of rent which a landlord can get for the flat and therefore reduce the potential level of profits from rented accommodation.

### Brief history of taxes falling upon rents

When Addington re-introduced income tax in 1803 he introduced the method of imposing taxes under five different schedules (A through to E). This arrangement was made so that each individual could pay tax upon different parts of his total income to different collectors of taxes, so that 'government' officials and Ministers would not know the total amount of income possessed by an individual taxpayer. Thus if a man had a total income of £1,000 a year, £500 deriving from houses which were let, £250 from the profits of trade and £250 from employment, he would pay tax under Schedules A, D and E. Each tax collector would deal with the incomes which fell within the provisions of one schedule and no one collector would know the total income of the taxpayer.

At first the payment of taxes under the different schedules followed general rules which applied to all schedules, but, within three years of the new arrangement being introduced, the Schedule A taxpayers were denied the right to deduct from their rental income the cost of repairs carried out to their houses. This meant that the effective rate of tax on the net income of the landlord was higher than that imposed upon other taxpayers. With the low levels of tax which were imposed in the nineteenth century, this unfavourable treatment of the landlord was probably of little economic consequence, but the precedent it set was of great importance. The reason for the amendment was said to be the fraudulent returns made by landlords claiming tax relief on repairs carried out by their tenants.

In 1878 recognition was given to manufacturers' need to depreciate their machinery and plant and a depreciation allowance was introduced. This meant that manufacturers were allowed to deduct from their gross profits the amount they had to set aside each year to cover sinking-funds on machinery with a limited life-span. This tax arrangement was  not extended to landlords, who still do not have the right to depreciate machinery which is installed in a dwelling-house.

If a landlord installs a sink geyser in a dwelling which did not previously have one, he is unable to deduct the cost from his current income because a geyser is defined as a 'capital' improvement. Nor may he depreciate the geyser over its lifetime. As geysers have a relatively short life (approximately ten years) this means that the landlord is unable on rent-controlled property to get back the capital cost of the geyser before the geyser needs to be renewed. When it is renewed, the renewal is defined as a 'current' repair and the cost may be deducted from current revenue. Thus at one time a geyser is defined as 'capital' and at another stage in the life of a house a new geyser may be regarded as a current cost of repairing and maintaining the dwelling. This arrangement means that a landlord of rent-controlled property permanently loses the value of the first geyser installed.

Depreciation allowances, which were introduced for manufacturers in 1878, preceded the landlord's right to deduct the cost of current repairs by sixteen years. It was not until 1894 that landlords were permitted a reduction from their Schedule A assessments in respect of the cost of repairs which they carried out. However, they were still not trusted to make honest claims and the amount which they were allowed to deduct was laid down by statute and was set as a fixed reduction of the Schedule A assessment. The reduction was one sixth of the Schedule A assessment and put landlords who did not carry out repairs into a slightly more favourable position than landlords who regularly repaired and maintained their property.

The system did, however, introduce something which might be informally regarded as a type of depreciation allowance. As the statutory reduction was fairly substantial, the amount of a sinking-fund as well as the cost of repairs would normally have been covered by the deduction. This rather unexpected benefit of Schedule A was lost when for tax purposes income from property was transferred to Schedule D in the tax year 1964–5. Later in this chapter an example is given of the present tax position of a housing association; the pre-1963 position of such associations would have been a little better than the position portrayed because the association could have deducted the Schedule A statutory deduction from its revenue. This would have meant that very little (if any) tax would have been payable during the first fifteen years of rent payment to the association. The statutory deduction was also high enough to allow some landlords of non-residential property a distinct tax advantage. The advantage arose because the 'deduction' greatly exceeded both the sinking-fund provisions and the cost of current repairs. However, this aspect of the old Schedule A system was seldom of much use to landlords of residential property.

In 1910 the system of a fixed reduction was modified to allow landlords who spent more than the statutory reduction on repairs to claim an additional maintenance allowance. However, the landlord's position was still unlike that of most other taxpayers as the landlord could only obtain the property maintenance allowance if the average amount spent on repairs each year exceeded the statutory deduction over a period of five years. As the calculation of income tax due under the other schedules was made on a yearly basis, the introduction of a five-year average basis for the landlord still left him in a more difficult position than other businessmen.

An example may clarify the landlord's position under the Schedule A arrangements which were in force up to 1963–4. If a landlord of a small rented house with a gross value of £40 spent £50 on roof repairs, his expenditure during that year would have exceeded the statutory repairs deduction of £10 by £40. In order to simplify the arithmetic, we can suppose that the landlord had spent nothing on repairs over the previous four years. His tax position in the year he spent the £50 would then be as follows:

4

| Annual statutory deduction | £10 |
|---|---|
| Total statutory deduction over five years | £50 |
| Total expenditure over five years | £50 |

As the total allowable 'deduction' equals the actual expenditure, the landlord would not have been entitled to any tax relief in the year in which the expenditure was incurred. If in the following year he spent a further £12 on repairs, he would then have been entitled to property-maintenance relief, because over the immediately preceding five years he would have spent £50 plus £12, which is equal to a yearly average expenditure of £12 8s. As this exceeds the statutory deduction of £10 by £2 8s., the landlord could claim a reduction of tax in respect of the £2 8s. If the landlord continued to spend £12 each year over the next three years, he would have obtained property-maintenance relief of £4 16s. two years after he spent the £50, £7 4s. three years after he spent the £50 and £9 12s. in the fourth year. Over a total period of nine years the total expenditure of the landlord would be £98 while the taxing authority would have allowed him a total sum of £114 for repairs. The landlord would not therefore have been overcharged with tax. However, the arrangement lacked a 'rational' basis and made it difficult to assess whether landlords were in fact more heavily or less heavily taxed than other income holders. Over a period of nine years their tax position was more favourable, but over a shorter period far less so.

The previous paragraphs describe the pre-1963 position of landlords. Rents will in future be taxed under Schedule D and landlords will now be able to offset current expenditure against current income in much the same manner as a manufacturer or trader. However, no provision was made under this Act to permit landlords to depreciate capital assets or to obtain an allowance to cover the wear and tear of equipment installed in houses.

At present, tax allowances of one sort or another are given on most properties used as part of a business. These include mills, factories or other similar premises, inland-navigation and dock installations, water, electricity, hydraulic power and tunnel undertakings, warehouses, mines, oil wells, foreign plantations, agricultural buildings (including tied cottages) and the buildings of the fish-catching industry. Houses are excluded unless they are built on a foreign plantation or by a mining concern, but sports pavilions may be depreciated for tax purposes provided they are erected for the 'enjoyment of the workers' of a factory. In general, the building of shops, offices or hotels cannot be 'depreciated'.

The tax allowances given to the owners of capital listed above are very substantial. First, an 'initial' allowance may be claimed for expenditure incurred in erecting, altering or extending an industrial building. This allowance is claimed in the first year and amounts to 5 per cent. Then an investment allowance may be claimed of 15 per cent. Like the initial allowance this allowance is set against income earned in the first year in which the building is in use. Finally there is an 'annual allowance for the wear and tear' of the building which amounts to 4 per cent of the capital cost of the building. These allowances can in total exceed the original capital cost of the buildings and they therefore represent a very real reduction of the tax liability.

The preferential tax treatment of industrial buildings can be justified on the grounds that the industrial capacity of the nation is vital to the national welfare and that capital should therefore be channelled into the building of factories rather than to house building. Clearly the productive output of the country is the vital factor in determining the national wealth and potential level of welfare. However a mere multiplicity of goods does not create welfare. Homes are also a fairly important element of economic and social welfare, and relatively few of the things particularly associated with the twentieth-century 'way of life' have much meaning without a home in which they can be used.

However, the taxing policy of governments since at least 1878 has been so designed that capital has flowed from rented dwellings into other forms of investment which rank for more favourable tax treatment. The return on rented accommodation has at times been sufficiently high to offset some of the tax disadvantages of holding money in houses, but with increasing levels of taxation the unfavourable treatment has become more serious. This is particularly true with respect to landlords who for one reason or another let dwellings on a 5 to 8 per cent return on capital.

The tax position of a housing association which borrows £100,000 and lets dwellings at a rent which is carefully calculated to cover all costs but to produce no 'profits' can be used to illustrate the difficulties confronting this type of landlord. Under the Housing Act 1961 the Minister of Housing and Local Government was given power to lend up to £25 million to *non-profit*-making associations. By 1964 the Government were satisfied that these associations could and should make a contribution to the solution of the British housing problems, and in the Housing Act 1964 a Housing Corporation was set up with powers to promote and assist the development of these associations.

The Corporation is at present expected to obtain funds totalling £300 million, which it will lend on forty- to sixty-year mortgages to newly formed and expanding associations.

The Ministry lay down rules regarding the organization and financial affairs of these associations and on many occasions Ministers of Housing have referred to them as non-profit-making. None the less they are subject to 'profits' tax and income tax, and the following example gives some indication of the burden which these taxes will impose upon the associations.[1]

### Tax imposed on a 'non-profit'-making housing association and the sinking-funds[2] of other types of private landlord

*Example*: £100,000 borrowed at 6 per cent interest, repayable over sixty years by equal annual payments of £6,188 to include principal and interest. The housing association has thirty dwellings.

Table 5 (p. 49 below) shows that during the first year in which the housing association collects rents, £6,000 must be collected to pay the interest. A further £188 must be collected and paid to the Public Works Loan Board which lent the capital of £100,000 on the contractual terms of an annual repayment of capital and interest. Income tax has to be paid on all 'profits', and as no depreciation allowance is given for dwellings, the £188 is defined for tax purposes as 'profits' and taxed accordingly. The tax on £188 is £72 17s. If the association collects exactly this amount from their tenants a further 7s. 9d. tax will be imposed upon each of the £73 collected. This means that the association has to collect more than £73 in order to pay the tax imposed upon rents which have been collected quite specifically to pay the tax imposed upon capital. The treasurer of the association must be left with £188 to pay to the lender and in order to have a balance of £188 he must collect £307. If he collects £307 and pays 307 times 7s. 9d. taxation (£119), he will be left with £188; if he collects anything less than £307 he will not be able to make the necessary annual repayment of capital to the lender. It is fair, therefore, to say that the tenants of a 'non-profit'-making association have to pay £307 for every £188 of the capital cost of their dwellings.

1. See pages 73 and 74 for the post-1965 position of housing associations.
2. The sinking-fund arrangements made by property companies are of particular importance in the case of properties bought on a long lease. Leaseholders cannot offset the absence of a sinking-fund against enhanced capital value of the plot, since such increases in value accrue to the ground landlord.

*Table 5: Annual rent needed to meet the debt charges of a housing association and the sinking-funds of other types of private landlord.[1]*

| Year | Expenditure | | Tax element | Annual rent per dwelling | |
|------|-------------|-----------|-------------|--------------------------|--------------------------|
|      | Interest | Principal |          | If no tax on sinking-fund | With tax on sinking-fund |
| 1 | 6,000 | 188 | 119 | 206·2 | 210·2 |
| 2 | 5,989 | 199 | 126 | 206·2 | 210·5 |
| 3 | 5,977 | 211 | 133 | 206·2 | 210·7 |
| 4 | 5,964 | 223 | 141 | 206·2 | 210·9 |
| 5 | 5,951 | 237 | 150 | 206·2 | 211·2 |

In the first year this tax puts up the net rent by £4 per annum. However, an examination of the first five years of the loan period should convince the reader that this tax will become heavier with every passing year. Each year the amount of capital collected and repaid to the lender rises, and with this rise the amount of taxation also rises. By the fifth year the tax element has risen from £119 to £150 for the association as a whole, and from £4 to £5 per annum for each individual tenant. After fifteen years the tax element rises to £268 per annum and imposes upon individual tenants a tax payment of £8 9s. a year. Table 6 gives the average position by five-yearly periods.

*Table 6: Average tax payments made in five-yearly periods (years 1 to 5, 6 to 10, etc.) and the average yearly rent.*

| Years | Average yearly repayment of principal | Average annual tax payment | Annual rent per dwelling | |
|-------|----------------------------------------|----------------------------|--------------------------|--------------|
|       |                                        |                            | Total | Tax element |
| 1 to 5 | 211 | 134 | 210·7 | 4·5 |
| 6 to 10 | 283 | 179 | 212·2 | 6·0 |
| 11 to 15 | 377 | 239 | 214·2 | 8·0 |
| 16 to 20 | 506 | 320 | 216·9 | 10·7 |
| 21 to 25 | 678 | 429 | 220·6 | 14·4 |
| 26 to 30 | 907 | 574 | 225·4 | 19·2 |
| 31 to 35 | 1,214 | 768 | 231·9 | 25·7 |
| 36 to 40 | 1,624 | 1,028 | 240·5 | 34·3 |
| 41 to 45 | 2,173 | 1,391 | 252·6 | 46·4 |
| 46 to 50 | 2,913 | 1,916 | 270·3 | 64·1 |
| 51 to 55 | 3,894 | 2,619 | 293·6 | 87·4 |
| 56 to 60 | 5,211 | 3,561 | 325·0 | 119·0 |

Total tax paid throughout period: £65,800.

1. All figures in this example have been rounded to the nearest pound.

Because the tax is imposed upon revenue collected to pay the tax, the effective tax rate on a housing association borrowing £100,000 is 13*s*. 2*d*. on every pound of capital. If an ordinary owner-occupier bought a house costing £3,300, the cost to the occupier of that house would be £3,300 plus the interest payments. For the tenant of any property purchased by a landlord for £3,300 the capital cost plus taxes raises the 'price' of the house to £5,530. As the tenant must pay this price in his regular rent payments, plus the interest on £3,300, tenants who can move from rented accommodation to owner-occupation have a very strong economic incentive for doing so.

It is worth very briefly noting here that not only has taxation been imposed to raise the 'price' of the house by taxing the capital value, but tax concessions given to owners (and not available to tenants) also have the effect of raising the spendable income of owner-occupiers. Thus owner-occupiers are favoured in two ways.[1]

The example given has referred only to capital repayments but it is also worth noting that, in the first years of a housing estate, housing associations have to accumulate a 'repairs-fund'. This is also subject to taxation and means that a tenant who has to pay £20 a year into a fund for outside painting, etc., has to pay a total of £32·65 to the landlord. The landlord can then put £20 into the repairs fund and pay the tax imposed of £12·65. Thus every tenant pays more for the repairs which are carried out in the early years of the estate than an individual who goes directly to a builder and pays the builder out of his current income.

Before turning to the taxes paid by individuals and the tax arrangements made to assist those who are purchasing a house on mortgage, a brief account will be given of the taxes falling upon the private landlord's main economic competitor, the building societies. On the whole the tax system has been more leniently applied to those lending to building societies than to other lenders. However, most of the tax concessions have now been removed and there is little tax incentive today for people to invest in the societies. As this was not always the case, a brief history of the taxation of building societies is given below.

## Taxation imposed upon lenders to the building societies

Collectors of taxes have always found it difficult and expensive to collect small amounts of tax from a large number of relatively small incomes. During the nineteenth century when tax was only 4*d*. in the pound, the administrative costs of collecting this tax from the majority

1. See the following chapter for a fuller discussion of interest payments and taxation.

of investors in building societies would have been very high relative to the tax return, as a large number of the investors had incomes below the tax limit of £150. Sorting out those liable to tax from those who were not could only be done with the co-operation of the building societies, but they resolutely refused to give any assistance to the revenue authorities.

In 1887 the Inland Revenue made a determined effort to obtain information from the societies but these were countered by the united opposition of all society spokesmen, who declared 'should it be known that such information is in any form given to the Inland Revenue, the effect would be disastrous to the business of building societies and lead to considerable withdrawals of investments therein'.[1] The Inland Revenue withdrew from the contest in 1888 saying at the time that their request for information had been made on the understanding that if such information had been given it would have been 'purely optional'. If the societies did not wish to co-operate the revenue would not press them.

However, if the collectors of taxes were defeated in their attempt to tax the individual incomes of investors in building societies, the Commissioners of Inland Revenue saw no reason why they should not make an effort to tax the members as a group by imposing a tax on 'profits'. This attack seriously alarmed the societies and in 1894 they made a voluntary agreement with the Commissioners. The agreement was an extremely simple one. Only 50 per cent of each society's shares, bonuses and deposit interest was charged to tax. By allowing 50 per cent of the interest to be untaxed the effective rate of tax which each investor paid was halved. This was a very 'rough and ready' method by which the low-income investors could obtain some of the tax relief to which they were entitled, and at the time it was not thought that many of the societies had investors with large enough incomes to pay the full rate of tax.

The Inland Revenue believed that they obtained the same amount of tax as they would have obtained had each investor been individually taxed. As, however, the societies paid the tax to the Inland Revenue, this department was saved a great deal of clerical work. In this first simple arrangement investors whose incomes were below the tax limit could claim repayment of the tax paid on their interest from building societies.

During the First World War this arrangement imposed a heavy burden upon those entitled to tax exemption or payment of tax at the

1. Price, op. cit., p. 488.

lower tax rates imposed upon incomes of less than £500 a year. Arrangements were therefore made in 1916 to tax the interest paid by the societies at 3s. in the pound instead of the full rate of 5s. In return for this concession the societies agreed that in future no repayment of income tax would be made against income derived from investments in or deposits with the societies. This scheme meant that investors with very small incomes below the taxable level had to pay a small amount of tax (3s. on 50 per cent of the interest received) on money they invested with building societies. The better-off investors, who would have paid the full rate of tax on other investments, paid less tax by investing in a building society. This arrangement was a private agreement made by representative officers of the societies and the Inland Revenue. It had no parliamentary sanction, and in view of the fact that it imposed extra tax on the poorer members of the societies it does not seem an arrangement of very sound social or democratic principle.

In 1921 the arrangement was renegotiated and agreement reached whereby the societies paid tax at half the standard rate on half the interest which they paid to investors. Or, in other words, those who invested in building societies paid a quarter of the standard rate of tax on every pound of interest received. For those who should have paid no tax this was an imposition, but for those who should have paid the standard rate it was a great incentive to invest in building societies. In 1923–4 the Commissioners of Inland Revenue asserted that some people and incorporated companies were investing as much as £50,000 or even perhaps £100,000 in order to benefit from this tax concession. In 1925–6 the agreement was modified so that those who invested more than £5,000 in the societies were taxed at the full standard rate. This stopped the flow of funds from companies merely seeking the preferential tax treatment.

However, this was an emergency arrangement and the Inland Revenue pursued the question of obtaining insufficient tax from investors in building societies very vigorously. In 1932, 1935, and again in 1940, alterations were made in the taxing arrangements. All the adjustments left the basic principle of a single lower than standard rate of tax untouched. The Inland Revenue continually refined their method of calculating the tax rate in an attempt to obtain for the Revenue the full amount of tax which would have been payable if each investor had been separately assessed. The taxing authorities ceased to be content to accept a rough approximation, such as the 1921 agreement which imposed an effective tax rate equal to a quarter of the standard rate. Each year the Inland Revenue calculated a composite rate which reflected the average amount of tax each individual would have paid if separately assessed. In 1938–9 this composite rate was $24\frac{4}{9}$ths of a penny, which was about 36 per cent of the standard rate of tax of 5s. 6d. In 1963–4 it was 5s. 5d., about 70 per cent of the standard tax rate of 7s. 9d.

The taxing arrangement by composite rate was given statutory authority in 1952. Throughout the history of this taxation the Revenue authorities have never been concerned with the question of encouraging or discouraging investment in building societies. Their problem has always been seen as one of obtaining the correct amount of tax. None the less the tax arrangement which has now been accepted has given an incentive to investors in the middle wealth ranges to invest in building societies. At the same time the arrangement has imposed an excessive tax burden upon the poorer taxpayers, who would (if they properly understood the tax arrangement) avoid investing in building societies. The wealthy investor obtains little or no tax benefit as he must pay surtax on the grossed-up amount of interest received.

In addition to the taxation of interest paid to investors, the Revenue also showed great interest in taxing the societies' 'profits'. The societies continually protested against such taxation on the grounds that they were 'non-profit'-making. However, in 1937 the National Defence Contribution (now the profits tax) was imposed on building societies. They were assessed on the same basis as other businesses, but were subject to the maximum taxation of $1\frac{1}{2}$ per cent of the earned surplus, this surplus being calculated before the deduction of interest payments. From 1947 to 1958 they were assessed on a basis applicable to limited companies, but the assessment was still subject to an overriding maximum. For instance, in the period 1947 to 1949, when the rate of profits tax was 25 per cent on distributed profits and 10 per cent on non-distributed profits, the building societies paid subject to a maximum of 6 per cent of their surplus. In 1956 to 1958, when profits tax was 30 per cent on distributed profits, 3 per cent on non-distributed, the building societies paid subject to the overriding maximum of 2 per cent.

In 1958 the building societies became liable to profits tax calculated on a basis exactly similar to that of any limited company. With the increase in the rates of tax, from 10 per cent in 1958 to 15 per cent in 1963, the societies now pay more tax than they would have done under the old agreement, which placed a relatively small tax on 'profits' calculated without deduction of interest paid on loans. Now, since building societies can deduct all expenses before calculating 'profits', these 'profits' are much smaller, but the rate of tax being higher the amount they pay has become greater per pound of profits. To summarize, the building societies have, by accident or design, obtained tax concessions since the nineteenth century which have been gradually whittled away but which were highly significant in the 1920s (the period when investment in building societies grew most rapidly), and they continued to have some advantage with respect to profits tax until 1958.[1]

## Conclusions

In this chapter it has been seen that taxes falling upon rented accommodation are heavy, and that, furthermore, they are heavier than the taxes falling upon many other types of building. This stems from the fiction in tax law that a 'house' lasts for ever and cannot therefore rank for any 'depreciation allowances'. Two most undesirable consequences follow from this fact. First, investors will not put their money into property as an 'investment', although they are willing to enter the property market as 'dealers' looking for capital gains. Secondly, tenants have to pay absurdly high interest rates on improvements to their accommodation. A 12½ per cent interest rate is exceedingly high, but this has to be charged on property with a life of twenty-five years to allow a landlord paying tax at 10s. 9d. on his sinking-fund instalments to obtain a 6½ per cent return on his capital. If there were no tax on the sinking-fund the tenant would only have to pay 9·3 per cent on the capital and the landlord would still obtain a 6½ per cent return on the original investment.

The taxation falling on the capital repayments of housing associations is very heavy and, unless the law is altered, housing associations cannot be expected to flourish. If a small association which only paid tax at 7s. 9d. owned a few houses costing £3,000 each, the tenants of the association would have to pay a total of £4,890 to the association to cover the capital repayments of £3,000. As such tenants also have to pay all the usual interest charges, management costs and repair costs, the heavy taxation seems certain to destroy the associations unless the law is very rapidly changed.[2]

Finally, it has been seen that the tax relief to building societies and

1. Finance Act 1965: building societies will be subject to the new corporation tax and, as things stand at present (written July 1965), to a capital gains tax on the sale of gilt-edged securities. The corporation tax leaves the building societies in a position comparable to other corporate commercial undertakings and continues the policy of treating the societies like any other profit-making concern.

2. Written in December 1964. See pages 73 and 74 for legislation introduced in 1965 to ease the position of housing associations.

their investors have been gradually whittled away and that very little is now left of the nineteenth-century concessions which were unwillingly given to these institutions. The tax policy of the country has been divorced from the housing policy of the country, and yet it has played, and continues to play, a vital role in the economics of housing and remains one of the main reasons for the decline of the private landlord. In the next chapter we shall see that it is not only the taxes imposed upon landlords but the combination of these taxes with concessions to owner-occupiers which have proved so disastrous to their competitive position.

# CHAPTER 5

# *Taxation and the Individual*

The previous chapter having dealt with the taxes which must be paid by landlords, in this one we shall consider the taxes paid by individual owner-occupiers, again ignoring local rates. As, however, it is intended to discuss the facts so as to bring out as clearly as possible the fiscal aid and assistance given to the landlord's main competitor – the lender of money to owner-occupiers – it is worth noting briefly that in the Report made to the Minister of Health in 1939 by the Departmental Committee on the Valuation for Rates[1] it was stated that dwellings built between 1919 and 1939 had been valued with reference to the valuations placed upon older houses. This meant that in the greatest period of shift to owner-occupation, occupiers of the newest houses were paying relatively less rates than the convenience of their houses would have warranted. Mr Walter Harvey in his reservations to the Report stated that 'statistics and evidence placed before us show that, speaking generally, post-war owner-occupied houses are about 30 per cent under-assessed'. If the statistics presented were correct, it would have meant that even through the rating system the landlord's competitive position was undermined during the crucial years when the building societies were being firmly established.

*Aid through income tax to owner-occupiers*

As the best available income-tax statistics relate to the tax year 1959-60, when Schedule A was still paid by owner-occupiers, it is best to start by examining the 'burden' of this tax upon owner-occupiers. With the abolition of Schedule A the burden has been turned into a more-or-less direct subsidy for all owner-occupiers who are buying their houses with the aid of a mortgage.

It is difficult to quantify the amount of assistance which the Government has given to the borrower for house purchase through the tax system. The tax arrangements only became significant to the owner-occupier when the high post-war taxation of the period 1919–39

1. H.M.S.O., 1944.

imposed a substantial burden upon a great many taxpayers. The Schedule A tax was imposed on the actual rental value of houses which were let and an estimated rental value of houses occupied by their owners. Originally, property was regularly valued, but the last complete revaluation of property for Schedule A was carried out in the years preceding 1936–7. All owner-occupiers were therefore paying Schedule A tax during 1945 to 1963 on the hypothetical mid-thirties value of the house and not on the much higher post-war values.

From the 105th Report of the Commissioners of Inland Revenue the average gross annual value of owner-occupied houses can be estimated. As would be expected, the richer the income earners the higher the valuation of their houses. In 1959–60 those in the income range of £180 to £1,000 were occupying houses which had an average annual value for tax purposes of £19 5s. to £22. The houses of those in the income group £1,000 to £1,250 had an average value of £24 4s.; in the £2,000 to £2,500 income group the average value was £39 7s. The average value of the houses occupied by the income group £8,000 to £10,000 was £91 4s.

These are the valuation figures for Schedule A tax and they are the amounts by which owner-occupiers had their income increased. It was thought that as these owners enjoyed a 'real' income from their houses, the income could and should be assessed to tax. However, before paying tax on this hypothetical income, owner-occupiers were allowed to make the same deductions from this income as private landlords. The first of these deductions was the statutory allowance for repairs. This allowance amounted to a quarter of the assessment if the gross annual value did not exceed £40. Between £40 and £50 the repairs allowance was £10 and between £50 and £100 it was a fifth. This allowance reduced the addition to the income of owner-occupiers earning less than £1,000 a year to an average increase of £15 to £16. For those with incomes between £8,000 and £10,000 a year, it reduced the average addition to income to about £73.

However, Parliament was not satisfied with the strange tax position of adding an estimated rental value (based on 1936–7 rents) to an owner-occupier's income and then deducting a part of that rental value to cover the cost of repairs. The tax circle was completed in a thoroughly 'Gilbert and Sullivan' manner by allowing owner-occupiers the same rights as the private landlord to deduct the full and true costs of all repairs carried out over a five-year period.

In the year 1959–60 only about 10 per cent of all owner-occupiers claimed relief of taxation on the grounds that their expenditure had exceeded the 'statutory deduction'. Table 7 gives the average Schedule A addition to the owner's income for all owner-occupiers and the average property maintenance relief claimed by those making a claim (only 10 per cent of the total). From this table it will be seen that the average relief claimed by the higher income group making a claim exceeded the average Schedule A assessment.

*Table 7: Tax 'burden' on owner-occupiers 1959–60.*

| Income range | Average Schedule A addition to owner's income | Average property maintenance relief claimed | Average taxable amount |
|---|---|---|---|
| £ | £ | £ | £ |
| *over*        *under*<br>1,000  to  1,250 | 24·4 | 23·2 | 1·2 |
| 1,250  to  1,500 | 29·3 | 27·7 | 1·6 |
| 1,500  to  1,750 | 34·2 | 30·5 | 3·7 |
| 1,750  to  2,000 | 39·7 | 37·4 | 2·3 |
| 2,000  to  2,500 | 44·2 | 40.4 | 3·8 |
| | | | |
| 2,500  to  3,000 | 50·6 | 46·5 | 4·1 |
| 3,000  to  4,000 | 56·9 | 63·6 | — 6·7 |
| 4,000  to  5,000 | 66·4 | 67·9 | — 1·5 |
| 5,000  to  6,000 | 72·9 | 160·0 | —87·1 |
| 6,000  to  8,000 | 91·4 | 156·4 | —65·0 |
| | | | |
| 8,000  to  10,000 | 102·4 | 185·9 | —83·5 |

The amount which was actually allowed against Schedule A for property maintenance relief could not exceed the Schedule A assessment. The five highest groups, which appear from the table to have claimed more in property maintenance relief than the average addition to their income, could not individually have done this. The figures could, however, only show a negative amount of income to be taxed if all those in the higher income groups with high Schedule A assessments claimed the maximum amount in property maintenance relief, while those with low Schedule A assessments did not bother to make any claim.[1] All the figures given are averages and they can therefore only show the 'average' position – on average the Schedule A tax was an extremely light tax, the reason for this being of course that the valuation of each house had been made on a mid-1930s basis.

1. Statistics supplied by Inland Revenue from their 1959–60 Survey of Incomes. See Statistical Appendix One, pp. 175–9.

In considering the position of the owner-occupier as portrayed in the above statistics, the reader might like to turn back to the position of the housing association landlord and reconsider in the light of the above table the 'burden' of tax laid upon such landlords. In comparing the two levels of tax it must be borne in mind that rented dwellings and owner-occupied dwellings held on mortgage are very close substitutes, and quite apart from any considerations of equity, if one is taxed while the other is not, purchasers of accommodation will all want to buy the untaxed house. Now that Schedule A has been abolished and the landlord is taxed under Schedule D his position has become relatively much worse while the position of the owner-occupier has become even more favourable.

*Tax allowances in respect of the payment of interest*

In a House of Commons debate on housing and urban land prices on 8 July 1963, Mr F. V. Corfield, Joint Parliamentary Secretary to the Ministry of Housing and Local Government, said:

'We hope, too, that together with the provisions of the Finance Bill, it [the government scheme to set up a Housing Corporation] can give a further impetus to the co-operative type of housing association in which the tenants and members of the association are the same people. Under this type of scheme, the tenant secures many of the *advantages*[1] of owner-occupation.'[2]

In this chapter we shall try to explain what these advantages are and to give some estimates of their monetary value.

When Schedule A was first introduced the majority of houses were let and the primary concern of the Government was to tax the rental income of landlords. However, many landlords were not freeholders and many had mortgages on their houses. These landlords had to pay a ground rent to the freeholder of the land and interest on the mortgage. Such payments were an expense which the landlords had to meet before they could benefit from the rental income of the house. Taxes were therefore calculated on the gross rent income which had been reduced by deducting any ground rent or interest payments that had to be made in respect of the property.

Private owner-occupiers, who paid tax on an imputed value of their property, were given the same right to deduct the ground rent or interest expenses which they had to meet. Until the late thirties, when the last valuation for Schedule A was made, this system worked fairly well. From a very narrow economic point of view the minimum rent of a

1. Author's italics.
2. Hansard, vol. 680, no. 142, col. 877.

house will be equal to interest charged at the current market rate upon the capital value of the house. For instance, if a house can be bought for £5,000 and the rate of interest is 5 per cent, the minimum rent will be £250. If the landlord is responsible for repairs and insurance a higher rent will be charged to cover these and management expenses. If property is regularly valued for tax purposes the valuation can hardly fall below the level of the interest return on the capital value. Therefore if a landlord or owner is taxed on such a value basis but has a 100 per cent mortgage on the house, no tax will be paid. For an owner-occupier it would mean in the example given that £250 was added to the occupier's income for tax purposes and £250 was deducted in respect of interest payments.

If, however, the valuation of houses is not regularly carried out, a house may be valued for tax purposes at £50 when the interest payments on the capital value of the house equal £250. For tax purposes this would not matter very much if interest could only be off-set against the assessed value, but under the tax laws of the U.K. such interest payments can be offset against any income. Thus landlords and owner occupiers can lower their general tax liability by the payment of interest. The private landlord has no incentive to do this. There is no business gain in making a loss just to avoid paying taxes. As the landlord is taxed on the actual rents he receives from the house, he has no incentive to make heavy interest payments on his houses.

Since the disruption of the First World War the owner-occupier has been placed in an especially favourable position. During the twenties and thirties new houses were valued with reference to the rental incomes of the controlled pre-war houses. Therefore the valuation was not an accurate reflection of the interest payment on the capital value of the house. Therefore a great number of valuations for Schedule A were below the interest paid on mortgages and thus the tax liability of the occupiers was reduced. During the last twenty years, when all prices have been rising very rapidly, the owner-occupier's position has improved year by year. Schedule A taxation has now been abolished, but owners have been left with all their old rights to deduct interest payments from their taxable income. The size of this concession to owner-occupiers can only be estimated, but the Inland Revenue have supplied some statistics from their survey of incomes made in 1959–60. Use has already been made of these figures to show the amount which owners claimed against the old Schedule A valuation in respect of maintenance costs (p. 58). We can now look at the amount which owner-occupiers claimed in respect of interest payments made to banks or

*Table 8: Interest claimed by taxpayers[1] in different income ranges.*

| Lower limit of income range | Average interest paid to building societies and banks | Percentage of taxpayers making a claim |
|---|---|---|
| £ | £ | |
| 50 | 56·9 | negligible |
| 100 | 56·2 | negligible |
| 150 | 52·8 | negligible |
| 180 | 57·2 | 1·7 |
| 200 | 57·1 | 2·1 |
| 250 | 49·7 | 2·6 |
| 300 | 44·8 | 3·3 |
| 350 | 50·9 | 4·6 |
| 400 | 49·4 | 5·9 |
| 450 | 47·9 | 7·3 |
| 500 | 47·4 | 9·4 |
| 550 | 48·3 | 11·6 |
| 600 | 46·9 | 15·2 |
| 650 | 49·1 ⎫ | 18·6 |
| 700 | 50·7 ⎭ | |
| 750 | 51·7 ⎫ | 21·1 |
| 800 | 53·1 ⎭ | |
| 850 | 54·5 ⎫ | 24·4 |
| 900 | 56·8 ⎭ | |
| 950 | 56·9 | 28·7 |
| 1,000 | 61·6 | 28·7 |
| 1,250 | 71·1 | 34·1 |
| 1,500 | 78·1 | 34·6 |
| 1,750 | 86·4 | 35·0 |
| 2,000 | 90·4 | 34·4 |
| 2,500 | 100·6 | 34·8 |
| 3,000 | 113·4 | 34·6 |
| 4,000 | 133·2 | 34·2 |
| 5,000 | 145·0 | 32·4 |
| 6,000 | 175·0 | 31·5 |
| 8,000 | 231·5 | 32·8 |
| 10,000 and over | 495·0 | 34·3 |

1. An 'individual' taxpayer is either a single person (single, widowed, divorced) or a husband *and* wife. The married couple is, for tax purposes, one 'individual'.

5

building societies. Not all the interest will have been paid for loans on house property, but by inspecting the statistics published by the Registrar of Friendly Societies it would seem that about 75 per cent of all interest payments made by taxpayers were made to building societies. Table 8 can be read in the following way. Nearly 29 per cent of the people with incomes in 1959–60 which exceeded £1,000 but were less than £1,250 claimed a reduction of tax in respect of interest payments to building societies and/or banks. The average amount of interest which these people paid was £61 6s. In the next income group (£1,250 to £1,500), 34 per cent of the people made a claim and they paid an average of £71 in interest to either building societies or to banks.

The total interest paid and claimed against income for tax purposes was £187 million, and roughly £140 million was paid in respect of houses mortgaged to private persons. Table 8 shows the *average* amount of interest claimed by taxpayers in the different income ranges.

These figures suggest several interesting things. First, the amount by which the average Schedule A valuation fell below the average amount of interest paid on houses bought during the late forties and fifties. On page 58 the *average* Schedule A assessment was given as £19 5s. to £22 for taxpayers in the income ranges from £180 to £1,000. The average interest paid by people in these ranges was £44 8s. to £57 2s. In the years since 1959–60 interest payments have risen substantially so that the tax relief granted now is greater than that suggested in the table.

The figures also show the uneven distribution of house ownership. At the lower income ranges very few people claim this particular tax relief, presumably because they do not own houses. The small number of very poor people who claim the relief are probably retired people who are still buying their houses, or perhaps a few temporarily unemployed professional people living on capital and bank overdraft.

The relative constancy of the percentage of people making this type of claim who have incomes over £1,250 is interesting and should be examined in conjunction with the next table (Table 9), which gives the data for interest payments to insurance companies. It seems probable that the constancy is mainly due to the increasing percentage of bank borrowers at the higher income ranges. On strictly commercial criteria we would expect the richer people to avoid borrowing from building societies as it is the most expensive form of housing loan for those who pay tax at the standard rate.

*Table 9: Interest paid to insurance companies, ground rents and other regular payments made by taxpayers and claimed against their taxable income, year 1959–60.*

| Lower limit of income range | Average amount claimed | Percentage of taxpayers making a claim |
|---|---|---|
| £ | £ | |
| 50 | 31·0 | negligible |
| 100 | 21·9 | negligible |
| 150 | 22·0 | negligible |
| 180 | 14·3 | 2·8 |
| 200 | 19·6 | 3·4 |
| 250 | 18·0 | 3·8 |
| 300 | 16·8 | 4·0 |
| 350 | 19·2 | 4·1 |
| 400 | 19·2 | 4·8 |
| 450 | 19·0 | 5·5 |
| 500 | 20·1 | 6·0 |
| 550 | 20·6 | 7·0 |
| 600 | 18·6 | 8·3 |
| 650 | 18·5 ⎫ | 9·8 |
| 700 | 19·8 ⎬ | |
| 750 | 20·6 ⎫ | 11·2 |
| 800 | 22·7 ⎬ | |
| 850 | 23·2 ⎫ | 12·9 |
| 900 | 24·6 ⎬ | |
| 950 | 26·1 | 15·3 |
| 1,000 | 31·7 | 15·3 |
| 1,250 | 46·3 | 20·8 |
| 1,500 | 59·2 | 25·8 |
| 1,750 | 75·2 | 29·7 |
| 2,000 | 92·0 | 33·2 |
| 2,500 | 119·5 | 39·0 |
| 3,000 | 157·1 | 42·5 |
| 4,000 | 231·5 | 46·0 |
| 5,000 | 291·3 | 48·1 |
| 6,000 | 344·2 | 53·8 |
| 8,000 | 522·2 | 55·0 |
| 10,000 and over | 1186·7 | 62·9 |

The figures given in this table do not relate to house purchase alone; they include any interest paid to an insurance company, a ground rent paid to a landlord, or payments, such as alimony, which are quite unconnected with housing. However, they are the best figures which the Inland Revenue can supply and it may be assumed that relatively few people are paying alimony. Some of the interest and ground rent will be for business premises; for instance, the interest paid by a doctor for the mortgage on a house which included his surgery would be incorporated in the statistics. Until more precise figures are supplied it might be assumed that about 70 per cent of the claims are made in respect of owner-occupied houses. This proportion has been calculated on the limited factual knowledge available.

We know that in 1959 British insurance companies had about £813 million out on private mortgage. In 1960 the amount rose to £927 million. During the tax year 1959–60 the interest on this capital must have been about £49 to £56 million. From the Inland Revenue figures we know that the total amount claimed as interest paid to insurance companies, ground rents and alimony, etc., was £98 million. The interest paid to insurance companies in respect of mortgages on dwelling-houses may therefore represent about 50 to 57 per cent of the total £98 million claimed under this head. A further £20 to £30 million may have been claimed with respect to ground-rent payments on leases of more than fifty-one years (but this figure can only be 'guessed' and no reliable data is available on which to found such guesses).[1]

If we add these figures to the £140 million of interest paid to building societies, we get a total of £210 to £220 million claimed by taxpayers in respect of interest payments made on their private houses. However, as a person's tax liability varies with his income and family circumstances, the tax relief given in respect of interest payments varies from family to family. Table 10 gives some indication of the extent of the variation.

The tax rates in the table are applied to different income levels. For *unearned* incomes the 7s. 9d. rate is applied to taxable income below £2,000, the 16s. 3d. rate of tax is paid on income between £10,000 and £12,000 a year. The highest rate of tax (17s. 9d.) is only paid on taxable income which exceeds £15,000 a year.

The *earned* income rates also apply to different income bands. The standard rate (7s. 9d.) was paid in the tax year 1963–4 on income below

1. Under the provisions of the Finance Act 1963 it will no longer be possible to deduct ground rent paid on long leases from personal income before assessing liability to surtax.

£4,005 a year and the rate of 16s. 3d. is not paid on earned income until taxable income reaches £14,000.

These tax arrangements make it extremely difficult to state the amount of tax relief obtained by a family whose income falls in any one of the income ranges. For instance, on page 63 the average amount of interest paid by taxpayers with an income of £2,500 to £3,000 is given as £119 5s.; if all the income was *unearned* this interest payment would lower the income tax paid by about £61. If all the income was

Table 10: *The amount of tax reduction obtained by taxpayers paying £100 in interest.*[1]

| Tax rate | Earned income[2] | | | Unearned income | | |
|---|---|---|---|---|---|---|
| | £ | s. | d. | £ | s. | d. |
| 4s. in £ | 15 | 11 | 1 | 20 | 0 | 0 |
| 6s. in £ | 23 | 6 | 8 | 33 | 0 | 0 |
| 7s. 9d. in £ | 30 | 2 | 9 | 38 | 15 | 0 |
| 9s. 9d. in £ | 37 | 18 | 4 | 48 | 15 | 0 |
| 10s. 3d. in £ | 39 | 17 | 3 | 51 | 5 | 0 |
| 11s. 3d. in £ | 43 | 15 | 0 | 56 | 5 | 0 |
| 12s. 3d. in £ | 54 | 8 | 5 | 61 | 5 | 0 |
| 13s. 3d. in £ | 58 | 17 | 9 | 66 | 5 | 0 |
| 14s. 3d. in £ | 63 | 6 | 8 | 71 | 5 | 0 |
| 15s. 3d. in £ | 67 | 15 | 7 | 76 | 5 | 0 |
| 16s. 3d. in £ | 81 | 5 | 0 | 81 | 5 | 0 |
| 17s. 3d. in £ | 86 | 5 | 0 | 86 | 5 | 0 |
| 17s. 9d. in £ | 88 | 15 | 0 | 88 | 15 | 0 |

*earned* it would lower the taxes due on the income by about £36. The actual amount depends upon the number of children and dependant relatives in each family and the amount of other allowable deductions claimed. However, the general principle of the tax is quite clear. The greater the income the greater the reduction of tax for every pound of interest paid and the more unearned, as opposed to earned, income which the taxpayer has, the greater the tax reduction.

As some people are reluctant to concede that an income-tax relief is a form of subsidy, Table 11 gives the 1963–4 tax position of two families. Each family is assumed to consist of husband and wife with

1. Tax rates for the year 1963–4.
2. In this table it has been assumed that the two-ninths earned-income allowance is obtained up to the 11s. 3d. rate. The one-ninth allowance obtained from the 12s. 3d. rate to the 15s. 3d. rate. From the 16s. 3d. rate the allowance ceases.

two children under the age of eleven. If one family rents accommodation and the other one is buying a house and paying £100 each year in interest to a building society, their respective tax payments for the year 1963–4 will be as shown in the table.

*Table 11: Comparative tax position of a family buying and a family renting a house (1963–4).*

| All income earned | Tax payment by (a) family who rents and (b) family who buys a house | | a–b=hidden subsidy |
|---|---|---|---|
| | (a) £ s. d. | (b) £ s. d. | £ s. d. |
| £800 | 10 0 10 | nil | 10 0 10 |
| £900 | 28 8 0 | 10 0 0 | 18 8 0 |
| £1,000 | 51 14 8 | 28 8 0 | 23 6 8 |
| £1,250 | 118 16 8 | 88 13 11 | 30 2 9 |

Before trying to identify the income level of the people who benefit most from this hidden subsidy, it is worth looking (see Table 12) at the way in which the tax allowance lowers the effective rate of interest for taxpayers in the various tax ranges.

To identify the people who benefit most from this tax arrangement we need to turn to the figures given at the end of this book in an appendix. The first two tables show the amount of interest actually paid by people in different income bands. By adding the interest up we find that 57·1 per cent of all interest paid to building societies and banks was paid by people with less than £1,000 a year (see Table A in Statistical Appendix One, page 176). However, from Table B of the appendix, we find that only 27 per cent of the interest paid to insurance companies, etc., was paid by people with an income below £1,000 a year.

At the other end of the income scale, over 25 per cent of the interest paid to insurance companies, etc., was paid by people with an income which exceeded £5,000, but only 2·9 per cent of building society and bank interest payments were made by people with incomes which exceeded this level. About 13 per cent of the total payment of £98 million paid to insurance companies, etc., was paid by people with incomes which exceeded £10,000.

Table D in the appendix gives the percentage of wives who were working. From this table it seems clear that many wives contribute to

*Table 12: Table showing effective rate of interest when the market rate is 6 per cent.*

| Tax rate | | Effective rate of interest | |
|---|---|---|---|
| | | On earned incomes % | On unearned incomes % |
| s. | d. | | |
| 4 | 0 | 5·07 | 4·8 |
| 6 | 0 | 4·6 | 4·0 |
| 7 | 9 | 4·2 | 3·7 |
| 9 | 9 | 3·7 | 3·1 |
| 10 | 3 | 3·6 | 2·8 |
| 11 | 3 | 3·4 | 2·6 |
| 12 | 3 | 2·7 | 2·3 |
| 13 | 3 | 2·5 | 2·0 |
| 14 | 3 | 2·2 | 1·7 |
| 15 | 3 | 1·9 | 1·4 |
| 16 | 3 | 1·1 | 1·1 |
| 17 | 3 | 0·8 | 0·8 |
| 17 | 9 | 0·7 | 0·7 |

the income of families buying a house. However, the fact that the family is buying a house rather than renting one does not seem to induce more wives to go out to work. Out of the 2,693,532 married couples paying interest to building societies and/or banks, about 39 per cent of the wives were earning. In the nation as a whole about 35 per cent of wives earned some income during the tax year 1959–60. In the higher income ranges (£950 to £1,500) a rather larger proportion of wives go out to work. This may be due to the fact that they are married to young men who are just starting their working lives and both husband and wife earn from £500 to £800 a year. Later, as the husband's income rises, there is a marked tendency for the proportion of wives at work to drop back to the national average and at the highest level it falls well below it.

*Amount of capital borrowed by individuals*

Table 13 gives (a) the calculated *average* amount borrowed by those who do borrow and (b) the percentage of people in each income range who borrow from either an insurance company or a building society. This estimate is made on the assumption that people do not borrow from both sources, but only from one or the other.

*Table 13: Estimated average amount borrowed by borrowers[1] (tax year 1959–60).*

| Lower limit of income group | From building societies | From insurance companies | Estimated percentage of individuals borrowing from one or the other source |
|---|---|---|---|
| £ | £ | £ | |
| 200 | 770 | 134 | 5·0 |
| 250 | 660 | 109 | 6·0 |
| 300 | 560 | 104 | 7·0 |
| 350 | 662 | 120 | 8·0 |
| 400 | 662 | 117 | 10·0 |
| 450 | 646 | 116 | 12·0 |
| 500 | 620 | 117 | 15·0 |
| 550 | 642 | 123 | 18·0 |
| 600 | 620 | 114 ⎫ | 23·0 |
| 650 | 652 | 112 ⎭ | |
| 700 | 662 | 120 ⎫ | 28·0 |
| 750 | 679 | 125 ⎭ | |
| 800 | 703 | 132 ⎫ | 32·0 |
| 850 | 719 | 140 ⎭ | |
| 900 | 750 | 153 | 37·0 |
| 950 | 751 | 163 | 37·0 |
| 1,000 | 812 | 190 | 44·0 |
| 1,250 | 940 | 279 | 54·0 |
| 1,500 | 1,031 | 356 | 60·0 |
| 1,750 | 1,160 | 453 | 64·0 |
| 2,000 | 1,182 | 561 | 67·0 |
| 2,500 | 1,350 | 725 | 73·0 |
| 3,000 | 1,472 | 949 | 77·0 |
| 4,000 | 1,745 | 1,377 | 80·0 |
| 5,000 | 1,956 | 1,731 | 80·0 |
| 6,000 | 2,431 | 2,066 | 85·0 |
| 8,000 | 3,114 | 3,075 | 87·0 |
| 10,000 and over | 6,450 | 7,092 | 97·0 |

These figures have been calculated on the assumption that the payment of interest is an accurate reflection of the amount of capital borrowed. The total amount of interest paid and claimed against

1. See the following pages for a full description of the way in which these figures have been calculated and their significance.

income has been divided among the income groups in accordance with the figures given by the Inland Revenue. The percentage of the total interest paid by each income group was then calculated. For example, 5 per cent of all interest paid to banks and building societies was claimed as a tax allowance by people in the income group £850 to £900. In the tax year 1959–60 the total amount of money which building societies had out on mortgage was £2,467 million; 5 per cent of this total is £123 million. By dividing £123 million by 171,053 (the number of people in the income range making a claim), £719 is obtained as the average amount of borrowed capital in the income range £850 to £900. The same calculation has been made on the estimated total value (£600 million) of private mortgages granted by British insurance companies to owner-occupiers of dwelling-houses.

These calculations can only give a rough approximation to the distribution of borrowed capital for private house purchase. Neither the building societies nor the insurance companies lend all the money they have out on mortgage to private individuals. The insurance companies probably lend quite a large amount to companies which build flats, offices, and shops to let. Of the £842 million which the insurance companies had in mortgages in 1959–60, about £600 million (approximately 70 per cent) was probably made to private individuals.[1] The building-society estimates must also be a little inaccurate, because it has been assumed by implication that payments of interest to banks are made equally by all income groups. This is obviously an incorrect assumption, and if it were possible to take the bank interest away from the figures supplied by the Inland Revenue we should no doubt find that the building societies lend rather more to the lower-income groups and less to the richer ones.

However, the figures are sufficiently accurate to reflect two important aspects of housing finance. The first is the relatively high borrowing of the richer income groups. The figures showing the percentage of individuals who borrow in each income group are by no means accurate, but they must nevertheless reflect fairly accurately the distribution of owner-occupiers by income ranges and the distribution by income of the mortgages granted by building societies and insurance companies. As the amount of capital available for house purchase is limited (and some of the borrowing at the higher levels is for tax-avoidance purposes), some of those who wish to borrow because they have no other way of obtaining adequate accommodation may find that funds are not available for them from the two major financial institutions which give

1. See *Board of Trade Journal*, 26 June 1964, pp. 1391–3.

mortgages. Both institutions are lending large quantities of their limited funds to people who may not strictly need to borrow. Such people would probably have a much smaller economic incentive to borrow if it were not for the tax concessions.

Many extremely expensive London flats and houses are sold to people who are faced with the unreasonable choice either of living in a heavily mortgaged flat or of contributing a large annual sum to the Exchequer funds. Almost anyone would select the first alternative, thus drawing capital away from other income groups and uses. It is therefore of considerable economic importance for the tax system to be examined to see whether this unfortunate choice cannot be removed from the taxpayer. There is no economic reason why some tax relief should not be given to everyone in respect of their accommodation costs.[1] There does, however, seem little justification for a tax arrangement which automatically gives a tax reduction on all the loan charges of a private dwelling. If interest paid on the land element of housing costs was excluded from the tax provisions, it is very likely that land prices would fall. This would be particularly likely in central residential districts where the very high capital cost of land can be offset by mortgagors who obtain large tax reductions on very heavy interest payments.

The second point which these figures illustrate is the shift from building-society mortgages towards insurance-company mortgages by people with incomes which exceed £2,500 (see Tables 8 and 9 on pages 61 and 63). This shift is almost entirely due to the preferential tax treatment of people who borrow from insurance companies. If a person borrows from a building society he is not entitled to any relief of taxation on the capital repayments of his loan, he only obtains tax relief on the interest payments. But if a person borrows from an insurance company he is able to obtain some tax relief on the repayment of the capital. The following example will show the extent of this extra tax relief.

*Example*: A mortgage of £3,500 for a period of twenty-five years at interest of 6½ per cent from an insurance company.

These mortgages are fixed for the full term, so the owner will pay interest on the full £3,500 throughout the twenty-five-year period. The interest will amount to £227 10s. per annum.

In addition a premium has to be paid each year on an endowment

1. See Chapters 9 and 10 for a fuller discussion of this.

policy which matures in twenty-five years, so ensuring that the loan will be repaid on the appointed day. If the borrower is thirty-five years old when the endowment policy starts, the annual premium would be about £153. This money can be regarded quite simply as the repayment of capital organized through the services of a specialist financial institution which not only invests the money at profit but also insures the life of the borrower. The insurance element is an extra advantage which insurance companies offer, but it does not alter the basic fact that the endowment policy is a simple and safe method of saving money in order to repay a loan. This type of saving is, however, regarded with special favour and Parliament has sanctioned a tax relief of about 3s. 1d. for every pound of premium paid. This tax relief is a little surprising when the endowment policy is one 'with profits'. From such policies the borrower may obtain a lump sum, when the policy matures, of about £5,500, which will leave him £2,000 in cash after he has paid back the loan.

*Table 14a: Account of the above transaction.*

|  | £ s. d. | £ s. d. |
|---|---|---|
| Gross annual interest | 227 10 0 |  |
| Less tax at 7s. 9d. |  | 88 3 0 |
| Gross Endowment Premium | 153 8 6 |  |
| Less tax at 3s. 1d. |  | 23 15 6 |
| Gross annual payment | 380 18 6 |  |
| Less tax | 111 18 6 |  |
| Net annual payment | £269 0s. 0d. |  |

*Table 14b: Account of the same transaction through a building society.*

|  | £ s. d. |
|---|---|
| Gross annual payment | 287 0 0 |
| Average annual interest paid £147 |  |
| Less tax on £147 at 7s. 9d. | 56 19 3 |
| Net annual payment | £230 0s. 9d. |
| NOTE: The difference in amount of tax relief per year (£111 18s. 6d. minus £56 19s. 3d.) therefore equals | £54 19s. 3d. |

As more of the people who have building-society loans have incomes below the standard rate of tax levels than do the people who have loans from insurance companies, the difference in the average tax concession to the two types of borrower is rather greater than the example suggests.

We have seen that the tax relief was not originally a subsidy to owner-occupiers. Their taxable income was increased by an imputed rent and then lowered by the actual costs of obtaining the imputed rental income. The element of subsidy has crept in more by accident than design, but like so many accidental developments it has much to recommend it.

First, the tax relief is easily understood and, given the rates of taxation, easily calculated. It is very easy to administer since, unlike most subsidies, it does not involve the actual payment of money – only the non-payment.

Secondly, for borrowers from building societies it gives the biggest subsidy when it is usually most needed. As the building societies are repaid some of their capital each year on the instalment type of mort-gage, the interest payment on the outstanding loan diminishes. Hence the size of the subsidy through tax relief also diminishes. If a family with young children bought a house on a twenty-year mortgage and paid interest on the loan of, say, £150 in the first year, the yearly interest would fall until in the last year it was perhaps £12 or £15. The tax relief would fall from £58 2s. 6d. in the first year to £4 13s. in the last year if the tax rate were 7s. 9d. in the pound. As the income of most families rises when children reach school-leaving age (perhaps ten or fifteen years after the house was bought), the diminishing subsidy seems a fairly sensible arrangement.

However, this benefit is lost when the loan is in the form of a fixed mortgage. As the interest remains constant throughout the term of the loan, so does the subsidy granted through tax relief. Equity between borrowers can only be achieved when the Government has decided whether or not it regards the diminishing subsidy as the most reasonable one. If it is thought desirable to allow a constant subsidy over the term of the mortgage, this treatment could and should be extended to the owners who borrow from building societies. This could be done by giving them the right to deduct from their gross taxable income the amount paid in interest during the first year of the mortgage (whether the payments made in subsequent years are in respect of interest or capital). The tax relief on insurance companies' endowment insurance policies is a part of a more general policy of giving encouragement to savers and need not be discussed here. However, in drawing up a policy of tax relief for owner-occupiers this element of the subsidy to borrowers from insurance companies should be remembered.

The Finance Act 1963[1] makes the following special provisions for housing associations formed by people who are co-owners of the property of the association. Such people are in effect at one and the same time landlords and tenants: landlords in that they have an owner-ship interest in the houses of the association and tenants by virtue of the fact that they rent one of the houses from the association. Section 43 of the Act provides that:

(a) rents to which the association was entitled from its members for the year or part shall be disregarded for income tax purposes, and

(b) any yearly interest payable by the association for the year or part shall be treated for tax purposes as payable not by the association but severally by the members of the association who during the year or part were tenants of property of the association, in the proportion which the rents payable by those members for the year or part bear to the aggregate of the rents to which the association was entitled to which interest relates.

The first sub-section (a) of this clause takes the co-owner type of housing association outside the taxing provisions which impose such a heavy burden of tax upon housing associations and other private landlords who let dwellings to families too poor or otherwise unwilling to be owners. The second sub-section (b) gives to the co-owners the other 'advantages' which ordinary owner-occupiers receive through the tax system. That these advantages are substantial cannot now be doubted. The tenant has not only to pay a higher rent in order to cover tax payments, he has also to pay that higher rent out of an income which is fully taxed.

As a result of the publication of the Milner Holland Report on Housing in Greater London in March 1965, a clause was inserted into the Finance (No. 2) Bill which will have the effect of relieving non-profit-making housing associations (which buy or build houses to let) from the burden of taxation to which reference was made in Chapter 3. The Act does not, however, exempt the associations from taxation, but it permits the Minister of Housing (in Scotland and Wales, the Secretary of State) to repay the amount of tax paid. Mr Robert Mellish, the Joint Parliamentary Secretary to the Ministry of Housing and Local Government, justified this solution to the problem of heavy taxation of non-profit-making bodies during the committee stage of the Bill's passage through the House of Commons by saying: 'The principle which it is desired to preserve is that, wherever a profit

1. See Mr Corfield's speech quoted on p. 59.

emerges, it should be taxed regardless of the arguments which might be advanced on social grounds for some assistance from the state.' He went on to say that the Government believed that 'if this principle were widely breeched, there would be no end to the claims for tax exemption on some ground or other for this or that body'.[1]

In this chapter we have already seen that general tax principles have been 'widely breeched' and that in the Finance Act 1963 the same problem was more neatly dealt with by simply defining the rents of housing associations of co-owners as rents to be disregarded for income-tax purposes. The two distinct methods selected for dealing with the same problem rests, it would seem, rather more upon the desire not to concede any tax relief to a private landlord than a strong desire to preserve tax principles. The difficulty of exempting housing associations which let dwellings from all taxes arises because such associations could be wound up and turned into profit-making landlords, if the managers of the association so wished. Thus a general exemption from tax might open the door to the abuse of the special status of a housing association. If this is the real justification for taking revenue from the associations in tax and then returning it to them by grant from the Ministry of Housing, it is unfortunate that the fiscal problem was not tackled by granting the associations and other private landlords the right to depreciate their houses over a period of forty to sixty years. If the rate of depreciation was identical to the rate of repayment of capital, the needs of the housing associations would have been met. Some slight difficulty would have arisen with regard to the valuation of private property, but such difficulties could fairly easily and equitably have been overcome by putting a zero value on all houses over sixty years old unless the landlord appealed against such a value on the grounds that (a) during the last ten years a substantial capital sum had been spent on the house which would preserve it for not less than thirty years, or (b) the house was of historic interest and had been continuously preserved for more than a hundred years. As most houses owned by private landlords are now over sixty years old, the valuation exercise should not overburden the Inland Revenue.

The serious disadvantage of the present system is that it once again introduces into housing economics an arbitrary element. It relieves tenants of a housing association of a burden of tax without doing anything for other tenants. It also appears to give the tenants of an association a continuing grant from the Ministry of Housing. Once such associations have repaid their capital, there seems no reason why

1. Hansard, vol. 714, no. 138, cols. 1711 and 1712.

some taxes should not be imposed upon any revenue collected in rents which is no longer required for the payment of interest or the repayment of capital. A very undesirable situation might arise after the repayment of the initial large loan used to buy land and cover building costs if housing-association flats or houses were let to friends of the management committee of the association at very favourable rents. The Finance Act makes no mention of the income groups for whom this special arrangement is intended, so that the arrangement could easily lead to the development of a new privileged group in the housing field. This cannot at present happen to the housing associations relieved of all tax by virtue of their charitable status, because they can only preserve that status by letting their houses to people defined as being in some type of special need.

*Conclusions*

The loss of rented accommodation can be explained by the development of building societies and tax provisions explained in this and the previous chapters. In view of the differential taxes imposed upon the two types of occupier, tenant and owner, it is not surprising that nearly everyone who has sufficient capital to become a mortgagor and buy a house has done so: 40 to 45 per cent of all households are now owner-occupiers and a further 30 per cent are living in dwellings which are owned by local authorities. As local authorities represent a 'competitor' to private landlords in the sense that they supply a product at a price below the level which could be matched by a private individual, the growth of local-authority housing since 1919 is considered in the next chapter.

# CHAPTER 6

# *Local-Authority Housing, 1919-39*

So far we have seen how by indirect methods government action has affected both the supply and demand for dwellings of particular types. In this chapter we shall consider the effects of direct government action on the supply of dwellings. Such action has restricted the private landlord in two quite separate ways. First, the action curbs and controls the landlord by imposing minimum standards upon him. For instance, early legislation prohibited the building of wooden houses in the City of London. As wooden houses were cheaper than brick ones, the prohibition made it more difficult for a private individual to supply dwellings at rents which the poorest families could afford. Secondly, the state subsidized one landlord (local authorities) and made the economic position of other landlords uncompetitive.

Little needs to be said about the first type of state 'interference'. There are now a mass of building by-laws and public-health laws which all tend to raise the supply price of accommodation. Both landlords and tenants have resisted legislative attempts to improve national housing standards, but the persistence of Parliament has finally forced landlords to recognize the authority of Medical Officers of Health and to calculate the profitability of housing in the expectation that public-health laws will be enforced. At first attempts to improve one aspect of housing standards were negated by the simple economic device of increasing the density at which buildings were used. Nineteenth-century overcrowding must have been partly due to the fact that brick houses cost so much that one family could not afford to occupy a whole house and the house was therefore let to two, three or more families.

The economic impossibility of providing well-built houses at rents which the poorest could pay led to overcrowding, which in turn led to legislative prohibition of high densities. Fire risks led to legislation imposing upon landlords the cost of providing means of escape from fire. With the development of modern plumbing and main water supplies, parliamentary attempts to get these supplied to every family presented landlords with insurmountable economic problems. The higher standards forced upon them either a reduction in profit margins or a total departure from the economic activity of supplying working-class families with accommodation. In the second half of the nineteenth century it seems that people thought that landlords' profit margins were sufficiently large to justify the imposition of higher standards. Landlords did not, however, view their economic situation in such a favourable light, and either could not or would not build to the higher standards which the public-health officials demanded.

The experience in Glasgow was fairly typical of the housing problems of the nineteenth century. A private Act (the City Improvement Act 1866) was passed to enable Glasgow to clear away its slum dwellings. This Act was administered with considerable vigour and in a period of five years several large slum areas were pulled down and 19,000 people were thereby made homeless. The destruction of the old slums was carried out in the interest of public health and, according to Professor Smart,[1] met with very little opposition. When, however, it was discovered that the families dishoused by the clearance schemes were not rehoused to the higher health standards required, people began to realize that such large dishousing programmes called for municipal rehousing programmes.

The Victorians were, however, very reluctant to move forward to this logical culmination of municipal action in the housing field. Economists and landlords argued very forcibly that if municipalities built houses to let at rents below market rents, private landlords would be forced out of business. The higher housing standards which were needed for public-health reasons made it impossible for either public or private landlords to clear slums and rebuild houses which could be let to the dispossessed ex-slum-dwellers at economic rents. The early legislation was a compromise between Victorian morality, which would not tolerate 'interference' with the free market system, and Victorian good sense, which was not blind to the economic fact that if people are forced to observe certain minimum public-health standards, someone will have to pay the price of the higher standards. Local authorities were permitted to build but severely restricted in the type of house they could erect. Glasgow, for instance, was first given power under special Acts to build one- and two-apartment (room) houses (flats). Under the most important of the nineteenth-century Acts (the Housing Act 1890) a local authority could not retain the houses they built for more than ten years without special permission from the Local Government Board.

The general reluctance to allow municipal building is clearly seen

1. *Economic Journal*, December 1904, vol. xiv, p. 537.

in the procedural difficulties which were imposed on authorities which attempted to implement the Acts. The Vestry in Shoreditch, for instance, resolved to clear away some of their slums in April 1890, but it was not until October 1899 that the first block of flats was built. The building of the block of flats took only one year, but eight years (from 1890 to 1898) were spent in negotiations and arbitration with the L.C.C. and the owners of the old buildings.

Under the early housing Acts, local authorities either rehoused the tenants on the original slum site which had been cleared or they bought cheaper land and, after clearing the expensive land, resold it. The Clare Market rookeries near the Strand were cleared in this way in 1902. Land was bought at Millbank, Dukes Court and York Street for the people dishoused from Clare Market. However, although the alternative land was cheaper than the Clare Market land, it was still too expensive for working-class people to pay economic rents. The value of the land was therefore 'written down'.

In this way the cost of the scheme to the local authority was represented by a once and for all loss. Millbank, for instance, cost £16,202 to buy; its value when used for working-class houses was £11,907 and this was the sum which was debited to the housing account. During the period 1902 to 1915 this particular scheme showed an annual contribution to the rate fund of £1,233. This 'profit' figure was calculated on the written-down book value of the land. Other estates showed losses even on the written-down value of the land. Such losses were met out of rates.

During the period 1890 to 1915 the London County Council bought under Part III of the Housing Act of 1890 and the later Housing Act of 1903 land to the value of £237,078. The written-down value of the land was £225,159 and the average annual charge on the rates was equivalent to 0·017 pence in the pound. Other authorities were making larger contributions to their housing accounts. Plymouth, for instance, was contributing the equivalent of 1·5 pence in the pound.

This method of subsidizing houses had several disadvantages. First, it tended to concentrate the subsidy in one year. The market value of the land had to be paid and if the value entered in the housing accounts was less than the amount actually paid for the land the difference had to be met by the authority in the year of purchase. The second objection to this method of subsidizing housing was that the full cost of any annual deficit in rent income fell upon the local authority. As few authorities were willing to undertake a business venture which might raise rates permanently, relatively few authorities used their housing powers. Those that did, did not rehouse the people dishoused from the clearance areas. Instead they rehoused the better-paid workers at rents which would cover the annual expenses of the estates.

This is brought out very clearly in the evidence submitted by Dr Mansfield Robinson, the Town Clerk of Shoreditch, to the Select Committee on Repayment of Loans by Local Authorities. He said that in Shoreditch out of 533 persons displaced in their clearance scheme, only one family could afford the rent which had been set. His evidence continues: ' . . . I believe that this is the same proportion as the County Council experienced in their Boundary Street scheme. I know they rehoused eleven families only out of something like 5,000 whom they displaced.' This situation arose even when the market value of the land had been written down from 11s. 6d. a foot to 4s. 6d.

The housing position in London during the period preceding the First World War is excellently portrayed by Dr Robinson in his evidence quoted at length below. Shoreditch was the only London Borough in 1902 to have completed a large housing scheme and thus the evidence of the borough town clerk is of particular interest. The evidence shows that all the same housing problems existed in that period which are still being discussed in parliamentary debates and the Press; the changes which have occurred in the nature of the problems are relatively slight. Now it is the West Indian immigrant who is most often quoted as causing overcrowding, whereas at the beginning of the century it was the Polish Jewish communities. Now families of three or four children have very great difficulty in finding accommodation and such families are those who most frequently become 'homeless'. In the earlier period it was families with six to eight children who found it almost impossible to get accommodation. And now the high price of land and the level of loan charges still causes the rents of council houses to be above the level which the poorest families can pay.

Dr Robinson's evidence to the Select Committee on Repayment of Loans by Local Authorities 1902 ran as follows:

*[Answer to] Question 5346*
We had a large number of applications. We advertised that the places were to be let, and we had about 300 applications for the first 50 tenements. We sent our superintendent round, and had a very careful report with reference to these people, and we gave preference to persons living in Shoreditch already persons who had been displaced by the scheme if there were any, but only one family applied. There was only one family, but perhaps three or four persons.

*Question 5350*
I do not think you have quite told us how you fixed on the one man out of 300 who was to enjoy the advantage of living in the house? – We had a

great number of applications from people who had such large families it was almost heart-rending to go through them, and that is one of the greatest evils of the housing question in the East End of London – people with 5, 6, 7 or 8 children would apply for two rooms; that is all they could afford from their wages, and we found that we should be allowing more than two people to occupy a room, and that, according to the Local Government Board standard, would be raising insanitary conditions; therefore we were bound first of all to strike out those who had larger families, and they were the bulk of the people. Now, those are the people who want housing accommodation in the East End of London; no private speculators will take them in because of the large families. We have had cases where people actually came and lied to us as to the number of their children, representing that they had a certain number, and when they got the tenements we found afterwards that they had other children who came up from the grandmother's house, or some relative's house, because they found they could not get accommodation if they told the truth as to the number of their family.

*Question 5441*
I take it that the people are being sweated in consequence of the scarcity of the houses? – Yes. I do not say that they do it wilfully to sweat them, but according to the economic principle of supply and demand, when there is all demand and no supply, then they have to pay a sweating rent. We have 30 per cent of workers in Shoreditch, and they are not Polish Jews and the wretched off-scouring of London, but the *bona fide* working man, who is the backbone of the country.

*Question 5446*
Is it not possible to carry out a housing scheme without charging for two rooms 7s. 6d.? – Not if you pay £21,000 for the land. We have come to this – that I am advising my council that it will be better to build municipal dwellings on leased land than on freehold land bought under these onerous conditions.

This situation called for drastic remedies and during the First World War promises were made to the electorate that the housing problem would be tackled with energy when the war was over. An election was fought on the slogan 'Homes Fit for Heroes' and in 1919 the first 'national' housing programme was introduced. The new programme can be simply summed up as an intention to build 500,000 houses for the working classes in a period of three years. It was estimated that the houses built in England and Wales would cost £800 each and those built in Scotland £850. The total capital cost of all the houses was expected to be £400 million.

It was thought from past experience that working-class families could afford to pay rents which would meet the costs of management and the payment of 3 to 4 per cent interest on the capital. Working-class rents were not expected to be high enough to produce a sinking-fund which would eliminate the capital loan over a period of sixty years. Thus the sinking-fund and (since interest rates were above 4 per cent) an extra subsidy of about 1 or 2 per cent would have to be given during the early post-war years, while interest rates remained high. These considerations led the Government to a belief that if a subsidy of about £10 million a year was given the working classes could afford to live in the new houses.

The actual building of the houses was entrusted to local authorities and public utility societies (which we should now call non-profit-making housing associations) whose 'profits' were limited to a return of 6 per cent on their capital. The Housing, Town Planning, etc., Act 1919, known as the Addison Act, gave local authorities the power to build houses to a standard approved by the Ministry of Health; all losses in excess of a 1*d*. rate were to be met by the Exchequer. This introduced a partnership between the local authorities and the central government. The greatest risks of the partnership were firmly laid on the central government, which would meet all losses after the local authority had made their maximum contribution of 1*d*. rate grant.

The public-utility societies were given a subsidy of 40 per cent of the loan charges on money they borrowed from the Public Works Loan Commissioners. As the societies were only permitted to borrow up to 75 per cent of their capital from the Commissioners, this subsidy was equal to a maximum aid of 30 per cent of all their loan charges.

These simple arrangements failed to produce the necessary number of houses and in 1920 the subsidies were extended to private builders. A lump-sum subsidy of £130 to £160 (according to size of house) was given to any builder who built a house for sale or rental. The subsidy was restricted to houses with a maximum floor area of 1,250 square feet but was not restricted to houses below a certain price, and no regulations were laid down as to the occupants of these houses. This provision was introduced with great reluctance, and in order to induce a rapid building programme the subsidy was only available for houses built within one year.

In 1921 Dr Addison (Minister of Health) announced an extension of the subsidy and its increase by £100 to £230; £280 could be given for larger houses of 1,400 square feet. According to the *Building Societies' Gazette* some confusion was caused in the building industry when the House of Lords rejected Addison's Bill, which would have made the increases operative.[1] By not passing the Bill the House of Lords terminated the first national experiment in subsidizing private-enterprise building. The policy had never been very popular and Sir A. Mond, M.P., summed up a prevailing opinion when he said in a House of Commons debate that 'between 25,000 and 30,000 houses had been

1. *Building Societies' Gazette*, 1921, p. 9.

erected under the builders' subsidy', and that many of the houses did not really come within the purpose of the housing scheme. About one third of the houses so erected were working-class dwellings and among the remainder were such houses as week-end bungalows.

In addition to the private builders' subsidy, Addison tried to induce more building by the public-utility societies by raising their subsidy in 1920 to 50 per cent of the loan charges payable to the Public Works Loan Commissioners. However, in 1920 the societies were unable to build for less than £1,000 a house and the revenue required to meet the capital charges was £60. With the current wage levels it was apparently difficult to get more than £20 per annum as *net* rent from tenants. The annual loss would therefore have been £40 and the subsidy was insufficient to cover this loss.

During 1921 both the Ministry of Health and the local authorities were trying to extricate themselves from a financial position which they found intolerable. At Newport, in Monmouthshire, houses which had just been built for £1,200 were being offered for sale at £625 with a reserved ground rent of £2 10*s*. At Bolton, houses which cost over £1,000 to build were offered at £600 with a ground rent of £3 10*s*. These sales were encouraged by the Ministry of Health provided they were restricted to sales made to members of the working classes.

The entire national housing programme petered out in 1922–3. Only a quarter of a million houses had been built under the various schemes instead of the half-million originally 'planned'. The reason most usually given for the failure of the Addison Act is the inflation which occurred in building costs. It is, however, very difficult to accept this as the true reason for the complete collapse of the national scheme. By 1923 small houses could be built for £600, which was £200 less than the 1919 estimate. The price of houses rose very rapidly in the years 1919–20 but fell with almost equal rapidity through 1922–3. It is, of course, obvious that there had been gross over-optimism in the original plan to build half a million houses in three years. However, to achieve the set target called for an extension of the time period rather than for the total collapse of the programme.

The estimated expenditure of £400 million on working-class houses was not in fact achieved until 1933. The annual subsidy which was met by the central government rose rapidly to £7 million for England and Wales alone, but it did not reach the estimated £10 million until 1928. If Scotland is included, the annual £10 million subsidy was first granted in 1927. However, it was thought by Members of Parliament and the public as a whole that if half the programme had cost seven tenths of the estimated cost, the total programme would exceed the estimates. As both Members of Parliament and the public tend to over-simplify economic phenomena, there is little doubt that they discounted the drop in prices which occurred in 1922 and assumed that, if the programme continued, houses would again cost over £1,000 to build.

The rise in the local-rate subsidy was perhaps of more significance in terminating the programme than the rise in the central government subsidy. The wording of the Act suggested that the ratepayers' contribution to the housing subsidy would be relatively slight and that the greatest burden would fall upon the taxpayer. This did in fact happen, but would scarcely bring much comfort to local ratepayers, whose contributions towards the cost of housing the working classes rose rapidly. During 1918–19 the rate subsidy to housing in England and Wales was £281,272; in 1919–20 it rose to £574,665, and by 1920–1 it had more than doubled to £1,231,341. It was not until 1921–2 that the rate subsidy fell, as the central government bore an increasing share of local losses. Even then it only fell to £1,106,836; in 1922–3 (when local authorities had started to sell their new houses) the rate subsidy fell to £836,237. This figure was more than twice as high as the 1913–14 rate subsidy (which had been nearly £400,000). One reason, therefore, for the rapid collapse of the whole programme may have been that experience showed local authorities that the 1d. rate contribution was more onerous than had at first been imagined. In this connexion it must be remembered that unemployment was high in both 1922 (14 per cent) and 1923 (12 per cent); at such a time ratepayers have no strong incentive to deal with the costly housing problems of their districts.

Another extremely important reason for the failure of the housing programme was the lack of integration in the government scheme to reduce the size of the National Debt and the local authorities' need to raise a capital sum of £400 million. Late in 1919 a Housing Finance Committee was set up to consider this problem and to recommend a long-term security which local authorities could issue for their housing needs. The Committee recommended that Housing Bonds of small denomination should be issued and that, as a special incentive to taxpayers, the first £100 of such Bonds should be paid without deduction of tax. It was felt that many local authorities would be able to raise the capital they needed within their own districts. If this failed the smaller authorities could go to the Public Works Loan Board while the larger ones could issue stock on the Stock Exchange. Thus each local authority was made responsible for raising its own capital and this financial arrangement has continued to the present day.

This Act has been examined in some detail because the seeds of all our present problems are clearly seen in the conception and failure of the Act. There was one clear objective – to build half a million houses in three years. But apart from this clearly comprehended aim there was little clarity of thought. When it seemed as if the programme would not be fulfilled, emergency action was taken to induce the building of houses for everyone and anyone. So for the first time the middle class obtained a direct housing subsidy and the needs of the working class were obscured by the dangers of subsidizing 'week-end' cottages.

There was a refusal or inability to co-ordinate the financial aspects of the housing programme with the national policy of deflation and the repayment of debt. Above all, there was a refusal to face the fact that house building is necessarily a long-term project and the output of houses cannot be increased with rapidity. Finally, there was a lack of understanding about the growth in the housing subsidies. At the beginning of any state aid to a social service, expenses will rise at an extremely rapid rate. Once the programme is established, the rate of growth of the subsidy will slow down. Unfortunately, in a democratic society the electorate is seldom willing to wait until a project is complete before calling it to a halt, as the costs double or even treble in the first two or three years.

A very brief history of housing legislation since 1923 will show the way in which government housing policy has shifted as different governments have obtained power and the economic situation of the country has changed.

*The Chamberlain Act subsidy of 1923*

1. Local authorities received a subsidy of £6 a year per dwelling for twenty years.
2. Public-utility societies could obtain the same subsidy.
3. For slum-clearance projects the Exchequer met half the estimated annual loss.
4. Private builders could also obtain a £6 a year subsidy or a lump-sum subsidy (instead of the £6) of £75. This subsidy was administered by the local authorities, who could add a subsidy from the rate fund if they wished.
5. This Act gave the local authorities power to guarantee building-society loans which exceeded the normal 70 per cent mortgage on a house which cost £1,500 or less to buy.

The most interesting aspect of this Act is its continuation of the Addison Act aid to private enterprise and, in effect, the middle-class purchasers of houses. In 1924 the Ministry of Health sent a circular to all local authorities reminding them that the subsidy was intended for the working classes and the total cost of a house which could receive the £75 subsidy was not to exceed £600. At the beginning of 1927 this figure was reduced to £550. In spite of these rather belated attempts of the Ministry to restrict the subsidy to the working classes, it is doubtful whether they benefited much, as the level of manual wages (about £120 to £160 per annum) did not permit many of them to buy houses.

The provision relating to building-society loans was clearly directed to the middle classes as a house costing £1,500 was well above the means of the working man of the time. However, the Small Dwellings Acquisition Acts were in operation and allowed councils to give mortgages of 90 per cent on houses up to £1,200 in value.

The second important thing to notice about this Act is the reversal of the roles of the central and local government. Under the Addison Act the central government bore the risks of local-authority housing. Each authority knew that its contribution to the housing account could not exceed a penny rate. Under the Chamberlain Act, the central government knew the extent of its liability while the councils bore the risk of losses in excess of the state subsidy. Sir John Simon explained the change very clearly in a debate on the 1923 Act.[1]

'Both schemes proceed on the basis of a partnership between the State, on the one hand, and the local authorities on the other, but this new proposal is a proposal of limited liability for the State, and undefined and, indeed, unmeasured responsibility on the part of the local authorities. . . .'[2]

Finally, the Act is important as it well portrays the optimism of those who think that the housing 'problem' will soon be solved. Neville Chamberlain's attitude at this time was that private enterprise was starting to build again. All that was needed was a little encouragement to local authorities to build while the private-enterprise side of the industry was still fully engaged in meeting the needs of the middle classes. Therefore all that the councils required was the smallest subsidy possible to ensure their co-operation during the temporary phase of continued lack of private-enterprise building.

The idea that private enterprise can and will supply houses for all families, if only the Government does not 'interfere' with the market, is a little strange when one has regard to the evidence given before the Royal Commission on the Housing of the Working Classes which sat in 1884–5, and the evidence given to the Joint Select Committee of the

1. Hansard, 25 April 1923.
2. See Statistical Appendix Two, pp. 181–4, on the variations of rate subsidy given.

House of Lords and House of Commons which met in 1902 to consider the 'Housing of the Working Classes'. However, it is a strongly entrenched opinion and there seems little hope of eradicating it.

It is, however, an unfortunate economic fact of life that if a government imposes minimum housing standards and permits vast numbers of people to crowd into small areas of the country, rents will rise beyond the means of the poorest 30 per cent of the population. As the population in a given area rises (as, for instance, in London, Birmingham, Brighton, Stevenage), the price and rent of land is bound to rise. If in addition to this increase in the cost of living the government insists that minimum public-health standards be imposed, landlords cannot supply new accommodation to families earning less than the average income.[1]

*The Wheatley Act subsidy of 1924*

A change of government shifted the emphasis of public-housing policy back to the local authorities, but the Chamberlain Act remained in operation. The most important provision of the Act was to raise the local-authority subsidy to £9 a year for forty years for the houses built by urban authorities. Houses built in agricultural parishes received a subsidy of £12 10s. The local authorities were authorized to make a contribution out of their rate fund of £4 10s. a year. The subsidy to public utilities was raised to £9, so keeping their subsidy at the same level as that received by councils.

Throughout 1926 there was much discussion about reducing the subsidies. According to the *Building Societies' Gazette* of 1926 the widespread fear among builders that the Chamberlain subsidy was to be cut unsettled the industry. However, cuts were not announced until 1 January 1927, when the Government decided to cut the Chamberlain Act lump-sum subsidy to £50 and the Wheatley Act subsidy to £7 10s. in the following October. Early in 1929 a further reduction in the subsidies was announced, but before they came into operation there was a change of government. Late in 1929 the Chamberlain Act subsidy was allowed to lapse though the Wheatley Act subsidy was continued at £7 10s. (£11 in rural areas).

It will be remembered that this period saw the most rapid growth of the building societies. In Chapters 3 and 4 we saw that this was the hey-day of the investor seeking a safe yield which was taxed with special leniency. In 1923 the amount advanced on mortgage by the societies was £32 million, in 1929 it was almost £75 million. The rate of increase in the

1. For the economic difficulty of building houses for families of every income group, see [L. E. Waddilove], *One Man's Vision. The Story of the Joseph Rowntree Village Trust*, Allen & Unwin, 1954.

total amount which the societies had out on mortgages was even greater. In 1923 it was nearly £99 million, but by the end of 1929 it was £268 million. This tremendous expansion put the societies into an un-challengeable position; most important of all, it gave them a constant stream of returning capital which maintained throughout the thirties the momentum which the situation of the twenties had created for them. The Government's action in subsidizing the sale of houses and the Inland Revenue's relative inaction on the tax question had by chance created a conjunction of economic supply and demand. The building societies were sufficiently established by the end of the twenties to become a permanent feature of the British economy.

The practical results of the housing programmes which were pursued between 1919 and 1929 are summarized in Table 15.

*Table 15: Dwellings built in England and Wales during the ten years 1919–29.*

|  | Total | Local authority | State-assisted private enterprise | Unassisted private enterprise |
|---|---|---|---|---|
| *Number built* | 1,274,588 | 467,524 | 361,137 | 445,927 |
| *Percentages* | 100 | 36·7 | 28·3 | 35·0 |

We do not know how many of the state-assisted private dwellings were for letting and how many for sale, but what evidence there is suggests that most of the private-enterprise dwellings were for sale. Neither do we know how many of the local-authority houses had been sold by 1930. However, it seems safe to assume from the above figures that between 1920 and 1929 about 37 per cent of all dwellings built were let, while about 63 per cent were sold to owner-occupiers.

The overall improvement in the national housing supply is suggested in the following statistics (Table 16) taken from the Census (England and Wales) Housing Report 1931.

*Table 16: Families living at more than 1½ persons per room.*

|  | Number of families | Percentage of families | Percentage of population |
|---|---|---|---|
| 1911 | 1,677,000 | 21·9 | n.a. |
| 1921 | 1,889,000 | 21·6 | 25·2 |
| 1931 | 1,636,000 | 16·0 | 18·7 |

The improvement between 1921 and 1931 is very marked and suggests that at least 253,000 of the new houses built were used to reduce overcrowding. As more than one and a quarter million houses were built during the ten-year period, about a million of the additional dwellings were used to raise the general level of housing. This pattern of allocation is roughly what could be expected in a free market. As new houses are built each section of the population benefits a little. In 1921 about 20 per cent of the population were rather densely crowded and presumably represented the poorest 20 per cent of the population. However, the poor, like the rich, benefit from a general increase in the supply of any commodity, and in this case they appear to have benefited roughly in arithmetical relation to their relative numbers.

These figures imply that the efforts of the Government were not effective in redirecting the market towards the provision of dwellings for the very poor. They do, however, show that the Government's general policy of encouraging house building had successfully seeped down to those most urgently in need. However, in 1931 there were still over five million people living at these high densities in England and Wales, and in Scotland the overcrowding was proportionately even higher.

## The 1930 Act subsidy

This Act attempted to redress the balance of housing policy. The Wheatley Act subsidy was continued for general needs, but attention was turned to the clearance of slums and a subsidy was given for each person rehoused from a slum. This subsidy worked out at about £12 15s. for a two-bedroom non-parlour house, £15 for a similar three-bedroom house and £19 10s. for a four-bedroom house. In agricultural districts the subsidy was a little higher (£2 10s. a person rehoused as compared with £2 5s. in urban areas).

The subsidy was given for a period of forty years and the Act introduced the idea of giving higher subsidies for tall buildings erected on expensive sites. The local authorities supplemented the Exchequer subsidy as in the 1923 and 1924 Acts.

This Act is noteworthy as the first to introduce a fairly complex subsidy and also because it is the first Act to encourage rent rebate schemes.

## The 1933 Act

This is an Act of minor importance, but it formally terminated the subsidies under the 1923 and 1924 Acts. It also slightly shifted housing policy back towards the needs of the better-off workers and lower middle-income groups by strengthening the position of the building societies. This was done by introducing a rather complex method of guaranteeing mortgage loans which exceeded 70 per cent of the valuation of the house. Both the Exchequer and the local authorities were involved in the guarantee of the additional mortgage. It was hoped that, by bringing in the Exchequer, greater use would be made of the 1923 Act provisions, which had not been used very much by local authorities. However, the councils did not like this scheme any better than the earlier one, and by March 1939 they had only 'guaranteed' 21,482[1] houses under the scheme.

## The 1935 Act subsidy

This Act continued the policy of the 1930 Slum Clearance Act by raising the subsidy for high-cost land. Its main provisions were:

1. Subsidy for dwellings built on high-cost land, all given over a period of 60 years – £6 per dwelling if the land cost between £1,500 and £4,000 per acre. An extra £3 if the land was between £6,000 and £8,000 per acre. An additional £1 was given for each additional £2,000 in the price of land.
2. The contribution of local authorities were made equal to that of the Exchequer.
3. In special circumstances a subsidy of £5 per dwelling could be obtained by authorities outside the high land cost areas. But this subsidy only ran for 20 years.
4. The subsidy to agricultural districts was for a 40-year period and was not less than £2 nor more than £8. The local-authority contribution was only £1.
5. Local authorities were permitted to consolidate their housing accounts.
6. This Act hopefully introduced a scheme whereby some of the subsidies could be returned to the central government. Any surplus made after 1940 was to be divided between the Ministry and the General Rate Fund in proportion to their contributions of subsidy.

This Act is interesting because, like the 1919 Act, it recognizes local-authority accounting procedure and sinking-fund arrangements, whereas the 1923 to 1933 Acts all had periods of subsidy which were considerably shorter than the normal period over which an authority amortizes its debt. In the nineteenth century local authorities were for housing purposes constrained to borrow on terms of thirty years,

1. J. R. Jarmain, *Housing Subsidies and Rents*, Stevens, 1948, pp. 25 and 26.

but in 1903 legislation was introduced to allow them to borrow for sixty years. In 1909 the period was lengthened to eighty years. However, private house purchasers borrowed for periods of ten to twenty years. The only reason for the sixty- to eighty-year sinking-fund was the impossiblity of accumulating the sinking-fund from working-class families in a shorter period of time. By the middle of the thirties the varying lengths of the different subsidies had introduced a high degree of complexity into local-authority accounts. It was clearly desirable for councils to plan their rent policy on a fairly long-term basis and if possible to avoid raising all rents at the end of the subsidy period. An equalization account was introduced into the council-housing account system to enable them to do this.

### The 1938 Act subsidy

This Act returned to the forty-year period of subsidy but raised the amount of subsidy particularly for high-cost land. On land costing £18,000 to £20,000, for instance, the subsidy was raised from £15 to £21. However, as the subsidy was for a shorter period of years, the benefit might be likened to a diet of jam today and no bread tomorrow. The most significant feature of the 1938 Act was that it saw a return to the earlier Acts of giving a uniform subsidy for all housing purposes, thereby reducing the emphasis on slum clearance.

This change of policy was made on the very reasonable grounds that the economic position of overcrowded families and families living in slums was the same, and that therefore the subsidies should be the same. In agricultural districts subsidies were made payable for houses erected for general needs as well as for those built to replace slums and to abate overcrowding.[1]

### Conclusions

During the twenty years 1919 to 1939 it was economically possible for landlords to build houses to let, but relatively few did so. Most of the new houses were deflected from the rental sector of the market because it was more profitable for builders to sell them and concentrate their economic effort on actual building. Many builders did, however, find that they had over-built for the owner-occupier sector of the market and they were forced to let their houses or sell them at a loss. Relatively few companies or individuals with money to invest invested in houses which they intended to hold as a long-term investment, but several companies invested in flats within the London region.

1. Nineteenth Annual Report of the Ministry of Health, 1937-8.

In assessing the profitability of any one investment, all alternative investments have to be considered. In the 1930s the rate of return on capital was so low in general that a gross 8 per cent return on property seemed very favourable. Such a return could be obtained on weekly rented accommodation which had been built before the First World War, but it could not be obtained so easily on newly built property which could be bought for owner-occupation because the building societies undercut the landlords. They gave 90 per cent (even sometimes 95 per cent) mortgages in the 1930s at 4½ per cent interest, and the total annual repayments of interest and capital came to less than 8 per cent simple interest on the capital.

In the next chapter we shall consider the post-war period, which has seen two important changes. First, during the period 1945–55 local authorities built for all and sundry, thus completing and consolidating their position as general suppliers of houses. Secondly, the high price of capital has made the competitive position of building societies even stronger, because if the landlord has to borrow at 6 per cent, he has to have a gross return of about 10 per cent to break even. This is a price which few people are willing or able to pay for the capital invested in the house in which they live.

# CHAPTER 7

# Local-Authority Housing and Government Subsidies, 1945-63

The national housing policy since 1945 has been remarkably similar to the policy of the inter-war period. The level of subsidies has altered but the principles upon which the subsidies are based have changed very little. Each subsidy is given for some specific reason and does not appear to have been directly related to the rent-paying capacity of tenants. The amount of Exchequer subsidy which is received by a local authority depends upon such things as:

(a) the age of the subsidized house;
(b) the cost of land;
(c) whether the house was built for an agricultural worker or not;
(d) whether the dwelling was built in a high or low block of flats;
(e) whether the houses were built as part of a slum-clearance scheme, or for the abatement of overcrowding or for elderly people;
(f) whether the dwellings are in a New Town or not;
(g) whether the house was bought to rehouse families when requisitioning ended between 1955 and 1960;
(h) whether the house was acquired and retained as 'temporary accommodation' under the Housing Repairs and Rents Act 1954.

Each new Housing Act which has been passed has been superimposed upon the existing subsidy structure, so that subsidies are now given under a dozen Acts passed between 1919 and 1961. No Exchequer subsidy has been retrospectively withdrawn although inflation has made it quite unnecessary to continue subsidizing houses built in the pre-war period at prices ranging from £250 to £400. Each individual local authority is permitted to pool all the Exchequer subsidies it receives and apply the total subsidy to all the dwellings in the housing account in any manner which the council sees fit. In general, English local authorities have transferred subsidies given under the older Acts from the houses built before 1951 and they apply these subsidies to dwellings built more recently.

The general principle is very simple. If an Exchequer subsidy of £12 per annum was given for sixty years for a particular house built in, say, 1934, this annual subsidy can be transferred to a much more expensive house built in 1964 upon which the Exchequer pays a subsidy of £24 per annum. If the house built in 1934 is let at a full-cost rent, the newer dwelling can be let at a rent which is £36 below the full cost. If inflation continues at its present rate for another thirty years, in 1994 the house built in 1964 can be let at a 'full-cost' rent and the occupier of the 1994 house can obtain the current 1994 subsidy plus the 1964 subsidy of £24.

This is the general principle, but in practice the principle does not work very satisfactorily. The bringing forward of the subsidy depends upon the building of new houses. If a local authority decides not to build any more houses it continues to obtain subsidies in respect of houses built at half the present cost of building, although the tenants could afford to pay an unsubsidized rent. Even worse, local authorities which did not build houses when they were cheaper to build, obtain an Exchequer subsidy which is too low to cover the gap between the amount the authority's housing applicants can afford to pay and the current economic rent for new houses. Thus at one and the same time some local authorities have more subsidy than they need and some less.

Another weakness of the present subsidy system is that it takes no account of the interest which is paid by a local authority on its total debt. This must not be confused with the current market rate of interest, which is the same for all authorities. The total debt of any one local authority is the result of many years of borrowing and building. An authority may, for instance, have borrowed money at 7 per cent in 1921, at 3 per cent in 1931, at 4 per cent in 1955 and at 6½ per cent in 1964. The length of each loan will be as variable as the interest rate and in any particular year the average interest paid on the total debt is a reflection of past rather than current borrowing. Thus an authority which has not undertaken much capital construction in a high interest-rate period may be paying an average rate of 4½ per cent on its total debt, whereas another authority which has borrowed when interest rates were high may be paying an average rate of 5½ per cent. As the same housing subsidy is given to each authority regardless of the authorities' current financial situation, this is another causal factor in granting more subsidy than is needed to one authority while granting less than is needed to another.

In this chapter a brief examination will be made of the existing level

7

of subsidies and the way in which they vary from authority to authority. Some of the variation appears to be quite arbitrary. However, some of the variation might be accounted for (and even be fully justified) by a detailed historical study of the housing accounts of each of the 1,470 English and Welsh housing authorities' accounts.

It has not been possible to carry out such a lengthy operation for this study and in this chapter use is made of the most readily available statistics. These statistics are published by the Institute of Municipal Treasurers and Accountants and give all the economic data necessary for calculating the aggregate size of the subsidy to each local authority. They do not, however, give sufficient detail to allow an estimate of the total number of dwellings which are actually subsidized.[1] For this reason all the statistics given in this chapter are averages. It cannot, however, be too strongly emphasized that not all dwellings owned by councils are subsidized by the Exchequer and that not all Exchequer subsidies are passed by the local authorities to the tenants of the particular dwelling on which the subsidy is given.

It is a part of the Government's policy that all the subsidies should be pooled and given to council tenants most in need. This means that some council tenants who are not defined as being in 'need' do not obtain a subsidy. The difficulty arises in defining 'need' and knowing how each separate housing authority defines need and distributes the total available subsidy among all the tenants.

Each local authority is free to set its own rents and to decide locally whether their tenants will pay rent according to the level of their individual or family incomes, or whether there will be one rent for all tenants of a single estate regardless of income. There are almost as many schemes for setting rents as there are local housing authorities, but inevitably each scheme has to take some account of the costs which the local authority has to meet. For this reason when measuring the size of the subsidy it should preferably be related in some way to the capital and/or the current costs of housing. An alternative approach is to relate the subsidy to the level of income of council tenants. This is impossible because we have no reliable statistics of council tenants' income nor, as stated above, do we know which tenants receive a subsidy.

From the data given below it will be seen that it is incorrect to divide all housing subsidies equally among all council tenants, as the Central Statistical Office in their estimates of the 'The Incidence of

---

1. Neither do they allow the reader to make a really confident division between a subsidy towards capital expenditure and one in respect of current expenditure. This problem only arises with reference to the subsidy from the rate fund.

Taxes and Social Service Benefits in 1961 and 1962'[1] have done. In this chapter the subsidy received by eighty-two[2] county boroughs and the thirty housing authorities in the former London County Council area are related to the capital costs of each authority's housing account. As the subsidies are given annually, the annual capital costs are the costs against which the subsidy should be set. These 'costs' are the 'debt charges'[3] and they cover all interest paid and repayment of capital debt. They are exactly equivalent to the mortgage payments which a private owner-occupier makes each year to a building society.

The primary purpose of this chapter is to make a comparison between the subsidies received by different local authorities and to see the results of forty-five years of uncoordinated housing policy. In each local authority examined the Exchequer and rate subsidy has been measured against £1 of debt charges. When an Exchequer subsidy is said to be 10s. in the pound (D.C.), this means that for every £100 which the local authority had to pay in 1962–3 to service its housing debt, the Exchequer paid to the local authority £50. The rate subsidy is measured in exactly the same way. By adding the two subsidies together we obtain the total subsidy, and from this we can obtain some idea of the relative amount tenants were contributing to their housing costs.[4]

Table 17 gives some indication of the differences which were found in the 112 authorities examined. The local authorities have been selected to show the great variations which are found in the level of subsidy in different towns.

Table 17.

| Authority | Exchequer subsidy per £1 of debt charges,[5] 1962–3 |
|-----------|------------------------------------------------------|
| Chelsea   | 12s. 1d. |
| Salford   | 7s. 3d. |
| Stockport | 5s. 6d. |
| Cardiff   | 4s. 9d. |
| Oxford    | 3s. 2d. |

1. *Economic Trends*, No. 124, February 1964.
2. All county boroughs are given in the 1962–3 housing statistics published by the Institute of Municipal Treasurers and Accountants (December 1963).
3. See pp. 181–4, Statistical Appendix Two, for subsidy to each county borough and London borough.
4. Where housing authorities pay lease rents an adjustment was made to allow for this factor.
5. For the sake of brevity, 'debt charges' are referred to as 'D.C.' in the rest of this chapter.

The five authorities given were selected for the following reasons. Chelsea, because it had the highest subsidy. Oxford, because it had the lowest. Salford, because it had the highest county borough subsidy, Stockport, because it obtained the county borough 'average' subsidy, and Cardiff to represent Wales. As land in Chelsea costs considerably more than land in or near Oxford, it is not surprising to see that the various Acts of Parliament which give subsidies for high-cost land and tall blocks of flats have resulted in Chelsea having a larger subsidy than Oxford.

However, this is by no means the full explanation. We are measuring the subsidy against debt charges but this is not the measure upon which the subsidy is actually given. As explained earlier in this and the previous chapter, the subsidies are given under various Acts of Parliament and in fact nearly all the subsidies are given as so much a year per dwelling regardless of the actual costs involved in borrowing and repaying capital. It is, however, true that the land subsidies take some account of the high annual debt charges which are incurred when high-cost land is purchased. Inevitably, if land costs £70,000 an acre the debt charges in respect of the land must be higher than the debt charges for land costing only £1,000 an acre. As the high land-cost subsidy is given over sixty years, this subsidy is used to offset the annual debt charges. Apart from the land subsidy, the subsidy on dwellings built by local authorities is a fixed amount regardless of cost.

In 1962–3 the average rate of interest paid by local authorities in London on their total debt varied from 3·95 per cent (Finsbury) to 5·16 per cent (Camberwell). If both Finsbury and Camberwell had built exactly the same number of dwellings under the same Acts, Finsbury would still have had a relatively higher Exchequer subsidy than Camberwell simply because of the interest-rate differential. In fact the two authorities did not build at exactly the same time and they will have received different levels of high-cost land subsidy. When all the historic differences are added together the resultant subsidy differences and cost differences were such that Finsbury obtained an Exchequer subsidy of 7s. 4d. a pound (D.C.) while Camberwell obtained an Exchequer subsidy of 5s. 4d. a pound (D.C.). This may be likened to a situation where an owner-occupier in Finsbury is entitled to deduct more from his taxable income than an owner-occupier in Camberwell in respect of a mortgage on identical types of house. Such a social policy can only be justified if it is thought that some people must live in Finsbury despite the high land costs.

If this is the reason for the higher than average Exchequer subsidies to boroughs like Chelsea, Stepney, Westminster, Paddington, Holborn and other central London boroughs, there seem good economic reasons for separately recording the land subsidies, because these are really given to industry and commerce and not to housing. If it is necessary for some workers to live in central London because of the nature of their work or to avoid overloading the transport system, the enterprises which employ these workers should pay sufficient wages to allow them to 'rent' the land upon which they live. It seems a little unreasonable that the general taxpayer should have to pay the cost of very expensive land because commercial firms wish to congregate together in central areas. If offices were more dispersed, land in Finsbury would be no more expensive than land in Camberwell and thus the housing subsidy to one authority need be no higher than to another.

The present lack of logic in the U.K. method of subsidizing dwellings is perhaps most clearly seen by comparing two neighbouring London authorities, Chelsea and Fulham. In 1962–3 the Exchequer subsidy to Chelsea was 12s. 1d. a pound (D.C.). The Exchequer subsidy obtained by Fulham was 6s. 3d. a pound (D.C.). The difference in the amount of subsidy given to the two authorities (when measured against debt charges) is partly due to the fact that Chelsea was paying an average rate of interest in 1962–3 of 3·96 per cent while Fulham was paying 4·83 per cent. This interest-rate difference 'explains' much of the difference between the two rates of subsidy, but it does not explain all the difference and it by no means justifies it.

The 'need' for an Exchequer housing subsidy in the two authorities might reasonably be measured with reference to the income of each authority and the amount of overcrowding, sharing and poor-quality housing. On all these counts Fulham appears to have a much greater housing need than Chelsea, as the figures in Table 18 show.

In addition to having a greater housing need measured by the census description of the stock of dwellings, Fulham also had less resources to meet its own needs. Its rate yield per person was considerably less than Chelsea's, and Chelsea had an additional small advantage over Fulham by having a slightly larger proportion of pre-war council dwellings than Fulham. By charging current rents for these older dwellings, local authorities are able to make some 'profits' which can be used to lower the rents of post-war dwellings. However, in Chelsea, as the Exchequer subsidy was relatively high, the average rent for these older dwellings was only 22s. 7d. a week while in Fulham the average rent was 34s. 3d. The average rents of post-war dwellings in the two boroughs were rather more equal; in Chelsea it was 40s. 7d. while in Fulham it was 42s. 2d. a week.

*Table 18: Comparison of housing subsidy and housing need in Chelsea and Fulham.*[1]

|  | Chelsea | Fulham |
|---|---|---|
| Exchequer subsidy 1962–3 | 12s. 1d. | 6s. 3d. ⎫ per £ debt |
| Rate subsidy 1962–3 | 1d. | 6s. 1d. ⎭ charges |
| 1d. rate yield per person 1962–3 | 3s. 4d. | 1s. 6d. |
| Persons living at more than 1½ persons per room 1961 | 3,430 | 11,400 |
| Percentage of dwellings without bathrooms 1961 | 11% | 31% |

*Table 19: Exchequer subsidy per £1 of debt charges, 1962–3.*

| Chelsea | 12s. 1d. |
|---|---|
| Kensington | 7s. 7d. |
| Fulham | 6s. 3d. |
| | |
| Islington | 7s. 11d. |
| Hackney | 7s. 8d. |
| Finsbury | 7s. 4d. |
| | |
| Paddington | 9s. 6d. |
| Westminster | 8s. 1d. |
| St Marylebone | 7s. 1d. |
| Holborn | 6s. 5d. |
| | |
| Southwark | 8s. 2d. |
| Deptford | 6s. 6d. |
| Camberwell | 5s. 4d. |
| | |
| Greenwich | 8s. 2d. |
| Lewisham | 6s. 6d. |
| Woolwich | 4s. 0d. |

1. Statistics from 1961 Census, London County volume, and I.M.T.A. housing statistics.

These facts suggest the full extent to which the housing subsidies have got out of line with current needs. Either the subsidy to Chelsea's housing account must have been too high or the subsidy to Fulham's housing account must have been too low. The two boroughs are so closely situated that in walking from one to the other no discernible boundary is passed and the incomes of the tenants of each of these authorities must be very similar because the whole of London constitutes one labour market. The difference in subsidy to Chelsea and Fulham is extreme, but an examination of Table 19 shows that other apparently unjustified differences exist between neighbouring London authorities.

*Rate subsidy*

Many local authorities subsidize their houses with a subsidy from their own rate fund as well as the Exchequer subsidy. Table A of the statistical appendix on p. 182 gives the rate subsidy measured against the debt charges for all county boroughs. In Ipswich, Brighton, Tynemouth and Eastbourne small contributions were made to the rate fund from the housing account but in all other county boroughs the housing revenue account either broke even or made a contribution to the account of sums ranging from 2*d.* to 6*s.* 5*d.* for every pound of annual debt charges paid. The Exchequer subsidy can be regarded as outside the control of the local authority but the rate subsidy varies according to the local councillors' assessment of the rent-paying capacity of their tenants and applicants. This subsidy therefore gives some idea of the local councillors' assessment of their tenants' needs.

Table 20 gives an indication of the variety of views held, the information showing that the variation of rate contribution is as great as

*Table 20: Rate subsidy per £1 of debt charges, 1962–3.*

| Authority | Rate subsidy | |
|---|---|---|
| | *s.* | *d.* |
| Bethnal Green | 10 | 11 |
| Chelsea | | 1 |
| Merthyr Tydfil | 6 | 3 |
| Eastbourne | 1 | 8 credit |

the range of Exchequer subsidy. The Exchequer subsidy varies from 12*s.* 1*d.* (Chelsea) to 3*s.* 2*d.* (Oxford), and the rate subsidy varies from 10*s.* 11*d.* to a 1*s.* 8*d.* credit per pound (D.C.). If the two subsidies are added together the variation becomes even larger than the two given separately.

*Table 21: Exchequer and rate subsidy, 1962–3.*

| Authority | Exchequer subsidy | | Rate subsidy | | Total | |
|---|---|---|---|---|---|---|
| | *s.* | *d.* | *s.* | *d.* | *s.* | *d.* |
| Stepney | 9 | 10 | 7 | 9 | 17 | 7 |
| Woolwich | 4 | 0 | 3 | 9 | 7 | 9 |
| Merthyr Tydfil | 6 | 11 | 6 | 3 | 13 | 2 |
| Eastbourne | 4 | 7 | 1 | 8 credit | 2 | 11 |

Table 21 gives both the highest and lowest subsidies obtained by the 112 authorities examined. Stepney and Woolwich show the extremes in London. Merthyr Tydfil and Eastbourne represent the extremes for the county boroughs.

The highest total subsidy of 17*s*. 7*d*. and the lowest of 2*s*. 11*d*. gives some idea of the complexities of the subsidy system and the danger of making any general statement about the level of subsidies received by local council tenants.

*A comparison of the two housing subsidies*

This is a convenient point at which to compare the 'subsidies' received by the two tenure groups, local authority tenants and private owner-occupiers. As a private individual buys a house on a twenty-five-year mortgage while a local authority buys on a sixty-year loan, a local authority pays more interest on the capital each year and less capital repayment than a private individual. However, as the average life of a private mortgage is in fact only about nine years, this implies that many owners sell their houses and move to another house before the full term of the first mortgage has run out. They then have a new mortgage on their second house, and by this process private individuals may well pay as much interest on their housing over a period of forty to fifty years as local authorities pay on theirs. This is particularly probable in a period of inflation.

If a local authority and a private individual both built houses in 1950 for £2,000 and the local authority had a sixty-year loan while the individual had a twenty-five-year mortgage, the individual would begin paying back large amounts of capital sooner than the local authority but if the individual sold his house in 1959 and bought a new one for say, £4,000 and had a mortgage of £3,000 on his new dwelling, he would then be paying more interest each year on his new mortgage than the local authority was paying on its 1950 loan. For this reason equating the 'debt charges' of local authorities with the mortgage payments of individuals seems to be legitimate and will permit a direct comparison between the tax-relief subsidy to the owner-occupier and the housing subsidy to local-authority landlords.

The owner of a house who pays income tax at 7s. 9d. on earned income obtains a tax relief equivalent to 6s. in the pound of interest paid. To allow for the subsidy element on capital repayment which is in- cluded in debt charges, a subsidy to local-authority landlords amounting to 5s. 3d. or 5s. 6d. would probably give a fair comparison with the owner-occupier. Thus those council tenants who obtain a subsidy (Exchequer plus rate) equal to or less than 5s. 3d. in the pound of debt charges can be fairly said to obtain about the same amount or less state aid than the average owner-occupier obtains in meeting any outstanding mortgage debt. Sixteen of the eighty-two county boroughs fall into this category and in Eastbourne the aid to council tenants (as a group) is only a little over half that which is given to many owner-occupiers.

A relatively slight change in interest rates can make a large difference to the relative value of the subsidy to local authorities. For instance, if the total subsidy was 10s. in the pound of debt charges, and interest payments amounted to £6,000 (subsidy £3,000) on a capital debt of £100,000, a change in interest rates of $\frac{1}{8}$ per cent raises the interest payment to £6,125. As the subsidy given under the various Acts of Parliament will remain at £3,000 the subsidy measured against debt charges falls to about 9s. 9d. a pound of interest paid. This is one of the more obvious disadvantages of the present subsidy system.

As the subsidies are all fixed, any increase in interest rates lowers the relative size of the subsidy at the same time as it raises the amount of revenue which the local authority has to collect from tenants or the general ratepayer. By measuring the subsidy per pound of debt charges, the effects of interest-rate changes are brought out very clearly. In Camberwell, for instance, the Exchequer subsidy was 8s. 4d. per pound (D.C.) in 1960-1. But because the average rate of interest which Camberwell was paying rose between 1960 and 1963, the Exchequer subsidy had fallen back to 5s. 4d. in the financial year 1962-3. At the same time the rate-fund subsidy to the housing account rose from 5s. to 7s. 5d.

Owner-occupiers do not suffer to this extent when interest rates rise. They do, of course, still have to pay more of their own income to pay the higher interest, but the tax relief remains at the old level per pound of interest paid and is worth more to the taxpayer. In this country a direct subsidy of interest rates has always been frowned upon, but in almost all other western European countries and the United States housing subsidies are given without financial disaster in respect of interest payments. By measuring the subsidy against debt charges we have seen that the U.K. subsidy system can be regarded as a subsidy given to meet the debt charges. However, the U.K. system has all the disadvantages of a subsidy tied directly to interest rates together with serious other disadvantages which are not found in any direct interest-rate subsidy.

*Housing subsidies as a measure of the real economic cost of large towns*

The housing statistics give some indications of the real economic cost to the nation of the concentration of population in London. If we assume that the subsidies are an accurate reflection of the needs of the local people, the height of the subsidies in London relative to the subsidy given in other parts of England and Wales strongly suggests the need for a complete and scientific costing of all local-authority housing. Within London the metropolitan boroughs have only been allowed to build within their own boundaries. This means that, before the reorganization of Greater London, Holborn, Westminster and boroughs like Stepney were constrained to buy high-cost land and to build blocks of flats which are taller than the most 'economic' height.

The London County Council, which was permitted to build houses anywhere within the county or the neighbouring counties, was not so confined and therefore supplied dwellings which obtain a lower subsidy than any of the other authorities mentioned above. In 1962–3 the subsidy to the L.C.C. housing account was in total 10s. 4d. in the pound of debt charges, and of this amount 5s. 9d. came from Exchequer funds. Although the Exchequer subsidy was one of the lowest in London, there were only two county boroughs (Merthyr Tydfil and Salford) which obtained a higher subsidy.

Tables 22 and 23 show the relatively high costs which the concentration of population in London imposes upon the nation. In 1962–3 the metropolitan boroughs obtained 8 per cent of the total Exchequer subsidy but had only 4 per cent of the total number of council dwellings. If the L.C.C. dwellings within the County of London were taken into consideration, the London share of the Exchequer subsidy would have been even more disproportionate. As each Act granting a subsidy has granted the same basic subsidy to all urban authorities, the higher subsidies in London must be entirely due to the very high cost of land

and building in the capital. Table 22 gives the percentage of one- and two-bedroom dwellings in each of the main types of local authority. From these figures we can see that not only do the London boroughs get two or three times as much subsidy per dwelling as the other authorities but these higher subsidies are paid on smaller dwellings. Thus, per square foot of habitable space, the subsidy in London is relatively higher than the figures per dwelling might suggest.

*Table 22: Average subsidy per £1 of debt charges by type of local authority.*

| Type of authority | Subsidy per £1 debt charges 1962–3 | | |
|---|---|---|---|
| | Exchequer | Rate | Total |
| | s.  d. | s.  d. | s.  d. |
| Metropolitan boroughs and City | 7  4 | 6  4 | 13  8 |
| London County Council | 5  9 | 4  7 | 10  4 |
| County boroughs | 5  6 | 1  9 | 7  3 |
| Non-county boroughs | 5  3 | 1  3 | 6  6 |
| Urban districts | 5  6 | 11 | 6  5 |
| Rural districts | 5  9 | 8 | 6  5 |

*Table 23: Average subsidy per dwelling by type of local authority.*

| Type of authority | Subsidy per dwelling 1962–3 | | | Percentage of dwellings with one or two bedrooms | |
|---|---|---|---|---|---|
| | Exchequer | Rate | Total | | |
| | £  s.  d. | £  s.  d. | £  s.  d. | One | Two |
| Metropolitan boroughs and City | 38  5  6 | 32 18  4 | 71  3 10 | 17 | 32 |
| London County Council | 22 10  1 | 17 10 11 | 40  1  0 | 14 | 43 |
| County boroughs | 16 10  5 | 5  3  1 | 21 13  6 | 9 | 24 |
| Non-county boroughs | 17  5  0 | 4  0 10 | 21  5 10 | 9 | 23 |
| Urban districts | 17  1  8 | 2 19  4 | 20  1  0 | 8 | 22 |
| Rural districts | 18  4  6 | 2  2 10 | 20  7  4 | 6 | 16 |

It seems possible that the housing-subsidy system has become part of the general lack of balance between the north and south of the country. Housing in London is more heavily subsidized than in other parts of the country and one of the main economic deterrents to large concentrations of population is lost. An example may help to clarify this point. Oldham in Lancashire and Stepney in London each have severe housing problems. In Stepney 10 per cent of the households were living in 'overcrowded' conditions in 1961 and many of the houses are in a very poor condition. In Oldham overcrowding is less acute but many houses are of a very low quality and defined as slums. In Oldham the average rent for a two-bedroom council flat was 22s. 5d. a week in 1962–3 and rents for these flats were in the range from 19s. to 33s. 5d. In Stepney the average rent was 22s. 9d. and the rent range was 15s. to 32s. 6d. The Exchequer subsidy in Oldham was 5s. 4d., when measured against the annual debt charges, and in Stepney it was 9s. 10d. Rate subsidy was 3s. 7d. in Oldham and 7s. 9d. in Stepney. Thus the total subsidy was 8s. 11d. in Oldham while in Stepney it was almost twice as high at 17s. 7d.

As the annual income of many families in Oldham must surely be lower than the average income of families in London, where employment is high, work opportunities good, and many wages tied to the London cost of living, it is difficult to feel happy about quite such a wide difference in the level of subsidy to the two local authorities.

As it costs more in real terms for a family to live in Stepney than in Oldham, the costs of accommodation should at least partially reflect this fact. If the wages of London workers were sufficiently high to cover their housing costs, employers of labour would have a greater incentive to move their work to other parts of the country.[1] At the same time workers would have an incentive to move to cheaper accommodation outside London. With the present chronic shortage of housing in and around London a drastic review of all subsidies might very profitably be made an integral part of any new policy for expanding towns and building new ones.

*Individual council tenants*

So far we have been looking at the figures of each authority and considering the benefits received by council tenants as a group. Council tenants, however, now have no right to a housing subsidy. It is their landlord who is subsidized and he may pass on the subsidy in any manner he chooses. Indeed, local authorities are no longer bound to pass on the subsidy. There is nothing to prevent a local authority from making a 'profit' on the housing account. Such profits are not real

1. For a more detailed discussion of this point, see Peter Hall, *London 2000*, Faber & Faber, 1963, pp. 97–103.

profits because they are calculated on the assumption that the Exchequer subsidy continues to be given. In Eastbourne, for instance, the tax-payers paid the local council 4s. 7d. in the pound of their debt charges in 1962–3. Out of this amount 2s. 11d. was passed on to the authority's tenants and 1s. 8d.[1] was passed on to the general ratepayers.

Many individual local-authority tenants do not obtain a housing subsidy and none obtain one by right, as do all owner-occupiers with a sufficient income. On the other hand, many individual local-authority tenants obtain a subsidy which is equal to or that even exceeds the total debt charges which accrue annually on the dwelling they occupy. We have seen that the variations in the subsidy paid to different authorities is considerable and we know that through differential and other rent schemes the subsidy to individual tenants of one authority is equally wide.

Most councils try to formulate a rent policy which will allow the poorest families on their waiting-list to rent council accommodation, but the little evidence which is available on this question strongly suggests that in places like London new dwellings are now priced beyond the rent-paying capacity of the poorest families. This would not be a matter for national concern if councils had sufficient very cheap pre-war accommodation to meet all the needs of their poorest applicants. Relatively few authorities are, however, in this position, and therefore, the lower-paid applicants stand in danger of being offered new accom-modation which is beyond their means. For these reasons authorities such as the G.L.C. raise the rents on their older houses above the historic cost level and use the extra revenue to lower the rents on their new dwellings. In this way the tenant of a new council dwelling derives benefit from three sources: the Exchequer, the ratepayers and the tenants of older council houses upon which the local authority is able to make 'true' profits.

This financial arrangement is economically justified and indeed very sensible, but for political reasons it is hard to implement. This is because it throws some of the costs of housing the present-day homeless and badly housed families upon existing council tenants. Council tenants are neither more nor less interested in rehousing the less fortunate families than other groups in society, and just as tax- and ratepayers complain about increasing taxes, so tenants complain bitterly of increasing rents. Council tenants, therefore, tend to exert political

1. Before the Finance Act 1965, however, this 'surplus' revenue was subject to the payment of income tax to the Exchequer. So that in a devious manner some of the subsidy was returned.

pressures to stop an increase in rents which will produce a revenue that is to be used to lower the rents of new dwellings. A substantial 'profit' rental income is in fact only collected by local authorities which have a sufficiently small number of local tenants to allow councillors to discount the loss of their votes. When rents are raised it is not usually with an eye to 'profit' but for the limited purpose of covering increasing current costs of repairs and management.

This examination of the average subsidy paid into different local-authority house-revenue accounts has shown that there is great variation between one authority and another. The variation is so great that no general statement can be made which would be valid for all local authorities or for all local-authority tenants. Some of the inconclusiveness of the prolonged political debates about the level of council rents may stem from this lack of uniformity. Any statement which is correct about one town in England may be completely incorrect if it is made without qualification about some other town.

### History of 1945–64 housing subsidies to local authorities

The remainder of this chapter will cover the history of British housing policy since 1945. In considering each shift of policy the actual level of subsidies given in 1963 should be borne in mind, as each individual Act is of relatively little importance. It is the cumulative effect of all the Acts which is the subject of interest. Looking at the separate Acts is like checking a route on a road map after going on a journey. The destination is already known, all that has to be examined is the route by which the destination was reached and the points at which something noteworthy occurred.

### Housing legislation 1945 to 1961

### Housing (*Financial and Miscellaneous Provisions*) 1946

1. A general standard grant of £16 10s. per dwelling for sixty years. The local-authority contribution was set at £5 10s. for the same term of years.
2. The subsidy in agricultural districts was £25 10s. with a local-authority contribution of £1 10s.
3. An additional subsidy of £2 a year could be claimed by authorities which incurred expenditure on rights of support, etc.
4. The Minister could reduce the rate subsidy if the amount of subsidy given in any particular district appeared excessive with reference to the subsidy being given by other authorities. If the Minister did reduce the local-authority contribution he was authorized to increase the Exchequer grant to make up the difference.

5. A review of the subsidies could be made after 1947.
6. Additional powers were given to the Minister to make loans to housing associations.
7. The subsidies for dwellings constructed on high-cost land were raised and a special higher subsidy scale was introduced for flats of at least four storeys in which lifts were installed. These provisions raised the subsidy on dwellings built on land costing £18,000 to £20,000 from £21 for forty years to £41 5s. for sixty years. When lifts were installed the Exchequer subsidy was £48 5s.

The subsidies given under this Act were regarded as being large enough to ensure that all local authorities could and would build houses to let at rents within the means of all prospective tenants. It is, however, interesting to notice that these subsidies only brought the subsidy to council tenants into line with the tax reduction claimed by owner-occupiers who built houses costing £2,000 on one twelfth of an acre of land. The standard rate of tax at the time was 9s. in the pound and if a private house were built on land costing £4,000 to £5,000 an acre and the money borrowed at 4 per cent (the rate of interest in 1946 to 1952) tax relief on the land could amount to, from £5 17s. to £7 13s. a year. If the building costs of £2,000 were borrowed, further tax relief of £36 could be obtained, making the total tax relief to the owner-occupier between £41 17s. and £43 13s.,[1] depending upon whether the land was just over £4,000 or just under £5,000 an acre. The Exchequer subsidy on land of this value was £30 and the local-authority subsidy £10, but if flats were built with lifts the subsidies were £37 and £13 10s. respectively.

*Housing Act 1952*

This Act raised all subsidies. The standard grant was raised to £26 14s. with a local-authority contribution of £8 18s. The subsidy for agricultural districts was increased to £35 14s. with a council contribution of £2 10s. Subsidies for dwellings built on high-cost land were raised, for example, to £54 9s. from the Exchequer and £18 3s. from the local authority for land costing between £4,000 and £5,000. These new rates of subsidy raised the assistance given to council tenants well above the amount of tax relief which owner-occupiers paying the standard rate of tax could have obtained. During 1952 the tax relief was

1. Tax relief depends on the income of the tax-payer; in this and future examples of tax relief to owner-occupiers an *unearned* income which is high enough to be taxed at the 'standard' rate of tax is used to calculate the relief allowed to the tax-payer.

£44 3s. 6d. and £46 1s. 6d. for a house built at the cost given in the previous paragraph. The subsidy for flats with lifts amounted to a total of £88 7s. a dwelling built on land that cost between £4,000 and £5,000.

## Housing Repairs and Rents Act 1954

This Act dealt primarily with rent control but gave local authorities power to buy old houses which could be made fit. The Minister was given power to meet half the annual loan charges (calculated on a sixty-year basis) or to make an annual payment of £3 for each separate dwelling. The definition of the type and locality of the houses which the local authority could buy appears to confine the subsidy to houses in clearance areas. In general, local authorities do not obtain any subsidy for existing houses which they buy either because the rents being charged are 'exorbitant' or to meet the general needs of the applicants on their housing list.

## Housing (Review of Contributions) Order 1954

This Order reduced housing subsidies to £22 1s. for urban areas and £31 1s. for agricultural districts. The local authority contribution fell to £7 7s. The subsidy for expensive sites was also reduced. For land costing between £4,000 to £5,000 the reduction was £47 8s. for buildings without lifts.

This fortuitously brought the Exchequer subsidy back into line with the tax relief to owner-occupiers, which had risen since 1952 because interest rates had risen to 4½ per cent. On a £2,000 house built on one twelfth of an acre of land which cost £4,000 an acre, the tax relief was £47 5s. If the land cost £5,000 the relief was £48 18s. 9d. However, council tenants received a further subsidy from the rates which still left them in a better position than owner-occupiers who obtained tax relief at the standard rate of tax.

## Housing Subsidies Act 1956

Summary of the provisions of the Act:
1. It reduced the subsidy for general needs to £10 a dwelling per year and relieved the local authorities of all obligation to make a contribution out of the General Rate Fund.
2. The Act emphasized the need for slum clearance, and the subsidy on houses built to rehouse families cleared from slums was maintained at £22 10s.
3. The Act retained the slightly higher subsidy which had been given since the war on houses built in new towns.

4. Flats received more favourable treatment. A flat built to meet general needs obtained a subsidy of £20 if four storeys high, £26 if five storeys high, and £38 if six storeys high, with an additional 35s. for each floor above six. Flats built for slum-clearance purposes were given an additional £12 subsidy.

5. The agricultural population was also favoured by being given a general needs subsidy of £19 instead of the £10 allowed to urban authorities.

6. The £2 subsidy introduced in the 1946 Act to help cover the costs of rights of support, etc. was raised to £5.

7. A new 'expensive site' subsidy was introduced into this Act. As with the other subsidies for high land costs the subsidy was varied with the costs of the site. For sites costing more than £4,000 but less than £5,000 the subsidy was £60 an acre. A further subsidy of £34 an acre was given for each £1,000 by which the cost of the site exceeded £5,000. Thus a site costing £7,000 (as developed ready for building) would obtain a subsidy of £128 an acre (£60, plus £34, plus £34). This subsidy was only available for 'approved' dwellings. (See paragraphs 2 and 4 above.)

At the time that this legislation was introduced into Parliament, interest rates on mortgages had risen to $5\frac{1}{2}$ per cent. The standard rate of tax was 8s. 6d. and the price of a house occupied by people paying the standard rate of tax on unearned income had risen to about £3,000. This meant that their tax relief on land costing £4,000 to £5,000 an acre (and built on to a density of twelve houses to the acre) could amount to £78 4s. for the £4,000 land and £79 18s. for the £5,000 land. If the occupiers only borrowed 75 per cent of the cost of their house, the tax relief would equal from £58 to £60.

### Housing Subsidies Order 1956 (S.I. 1956, No. 2015)

This Order abolished the 'general needs' Exchequer subsidy but retained it for dwellings of not more than one bedroom, thus introducing the special subsidy arrangement for old people's dwellings.

### Housing (Financial Provisions) Act 1958

This Act confirmed the Government's attitude to houses built to meet the 'general needs' of the country by providing a nominal subsidy of 1s. a year for dwellings required by:

1. The agricultural population.

8

2. Dwellings in which the costs were substantially enhanced by securing protection against the consequences of a subsidence of the site.
3. Dwellings which were built when more housing accommodation was 'urgently needed'.

This very low subsidy could, however, be increased at the Minister's discretion by £9 in the case of agricultural dwellings and up to £30 for houses built in areas of special financial need. Flats in higher blocks could, at the Minister's discretion, be given a subsidy of £40 a flat. Apart from this provision the Act made little change in the rates of subsidy provided for designated purpose, such as slum clearance, laid down by the 1956 Act. The expensive-site subsidy was retained at its old level, although by 1958 rates of interest had risen to 6 per cent so that the tax relief to owner-occupiers had further increased.

These subsidies remained in force until 1961, when the Government reintroduced a general-needs subsidy and recast the subsidies in a determined attempt to force local authorities to charge rents comparable to those set for the tenants of private landlords by the Rent Act, 1957.

*Housing Act 1961*

*Amount of subsidy*

1. Dwellings provided for special purposes.
   (a) Town development and comprehensive development similar to a new Town    £28
   (b) For the urgent needs of industry    £24
2. (a) Other approved needs, i.e. slum clearance, overcrowding, and general needs    £24 or £8
   (b) Approved dwellings provided by housing associations    £24
   (c) Local authorities whose resources are particularly deficient when viewed in terms of the yield of 1*d*. rate up to    £40
   (d) Flats in blocks of four storeys to have an additional subsidy as follows:
   Four storeys    £8
   Five storeys    £14
   Six storeys    £26
   For higher blocks of flats    £26 plus 35*s*. for each additional storey

3. The subsidy on expensive sites and agricultural dwellings remained unchanged.

The most important provision of this Act is the alternative subsidy given under 2(a) above. The Minister wished the local authorities to charge rents equal to twice the gross annual value of their dwellings. He therefore provided the higher subsidy for those councils which were unable to balance their housing accounts even if they charged rents calculated on the gross annual value[1] of each dwelling. If a council could obtain a large enough income to obtain a favourable balance on their housing account by charging rents equal to twice the gross value, they only qualified for a subsidy of £8. Each authority has to draw up the following account for the Minister:

| *Income* | *Expenditure* |
|---|---|
| Assumed rental income of twice the gross value of all the council's dwellings, | Loan charges, *plus* repairs, *plus* management. |
| *plus* all Exchequer subsidies, *plus* any other income. | |
| These items give TOTAL INCOME. | These items give TOTAL EXPENDITURE. |

If the assumed income exceeds the expenditure during the year preceding the completion of the council houses to be subsidized, the subsidy is £8. If expenditure exceeds income, the full subsidy of £24 is given. This device is known as a 'resource' test; presumably because it is some test of the resourcefulness of borough treasurers in ensuring that economies are not practised in the management of council property if such economies would result in expenditure being less than income. The Act might well be renamed, 'The Incitement to Extra Expenditure Act, 1961'.

One of the side-effects of the 1961 Act is that it will tend to discourage council building for large families, still one of the most badly housed groups in our society. A large house will necessarily have a larger annual gross value than a small house, but there is every reason to suppose that a large family will not be able to afford as large a rent as a small family. By calculating future subsidies on a hypothetical income derived from gross values, the Minister is penalizing the local

---

1. 'Gross annual value' is a valuation imposed upon houses for tax purposes. The 1957 Rent Act permitted rent increases to twice the gross value.

authority which builds large houses and lets them to the poorest large families of the district at rents within their means.

The brief history given in these two chapters shows how relatively slow the increase in subsidy payments has been since 1930. The general rise in prices has far outstripped the Exchequer subsidy. In 1930 the subsidy was £11 5s. for a three-bedroom dwelling and in 1964 it was £24. Over the same period the cost of building a house rose from about £350 to about £2,100 (excluding land), an increase of six times compared with the subsidy increase of just over two times.

The primary object in discussing the local authorities as landlords has been to assess their potential power as a competitor to private landlords. In Chapter 9 a fuller discussion of the role of local authorities as distributors of subsidies to tenants will be given.

The private landlord is not merely left out of the subsidy arrangements, he is also heavily taxed on any revenue he has to collect for sinking-fund purposes. The examination of the two forms of subsidy (income-tax relief and direct subsidies to local authorities) together with the taxes which fall upon landlords, leads inevitably to the conclusion that the competitive economic position of private landlords has been completely undermined since 1919. On the facts so far discussed few economists would have expected the private landlord to have survived the last forty-five years. The private landlord does, however, still supply 30 per cent of all dwellings, and the reason for his survival is not difficult to find.

Rent controls have for long been accepted as the economic cause for the decline of the private landlord. They seem, however, to have operated more strongly as a method of keeping landlords in business. They have not made landlords 'willing' to remain in business but they have effectively made the cost of exit from the economic function of supplying accommodation very high. Over at least the last thirty years landlords of rent-controlled property have had more reason to retain their property than landlords of decontrolled or uncontrolled property. The economic reason for this apparent paradox will be explained in the next chapter.

CHAPTER 8

# Rent Control

*The general effects of price control*

In general it is quite certain that if the price of a commodity is fixed by law below the free market price, the supply of that commodity will be reduced. If, for instance, the free market price of a cotton sheet is £1 and the price is controlled at 15s., we can predict with almost complete certainty that fewer cotton sheets will be manufactured and made available for sale. The low price will reduce the profits of everyone who makes and sells sheets, and manufacturers will be less willing to make them and wholesalers and retailers less willing to stock them. As cotton sheets do not take long to manufacture, within a year of such price controls the supply of sheets will be reduced sufficiently for consumers to complain of a 'shortage' of sheets. Factories will have shifted their production to other products which are not price controlled, and while cotton sheets are in short supply there could easily be a surplus of other cotton goods which are not price controlled.

In the supply of dwellings the same principles apply, and if the 'price' or 'rent' of dwellings is controlled below the market price fewer dwellings will be supplied. However, as dwellings take an extremely long time to 'produce' price control cannot immediately lower the supply of dwellings to any noticeable extent. At any given moment of time 98 per cent of all dwellings are not being 'made', they are already built. Of those which are built, about 98 per cent have already been occupied when rent controls are introduced. Thus 96 per cent of the total national stock of dwellings have been 'made' and are 'occupied' when rent control is introduced. If we think of a landlord as an ordinary businessman supplying a saleable commodity, the most important aspect of rent control centres around the methods which landlords use to escape from the disliked consequences of price controls.

One of the things the landlord could do is pull down his houses and build on the land something which is not 'controlled'. The U.K. legislation controlling rents has effectively prevented most landlords from doing this, but even if landlords had been given the right to evict tenants when they wished to demolish a rent-controlled house, it would not have been profitable for all landlords to do so. If we think of the total land area of London, it is surely obvious that only a small proportion of the land now occupied by dwellings could be profitably turned over to shop or office use. If all the dwellings in Westminster, for example, were taken down and all the land used for offices, there would be a very much reduced demand for office space in Paddington and St Marylebone. The profits gained from offices would fall. At the same time, because about 33,000 families in Westminster would have been made 'homeless', the potential profits which could be obtained by supplying dwellings would rise and landlords would lose the incentive to pull down their houses.

The control of rents would not allow landlords to obtain the higher profits immediately, but so long as landlords think that rent controls will be removed in about five years time, some landlords can be found willing to invest in dwellings as a long-term project. Such landlords will, however, make a very careful selection of the areas in which they invest. Their main interest is in the future and they require a fairly certain future to induce them to undertake all the risks involved. Only an expert, with a flair for prediction and some of the psychological attitudes of a gambler, can bring off the really big and highly profitable successes in residential property dealings. Many company directors with very staid financial policies can, however, see the prospects for future property development in residential areas which are situated fairly near the centre of a town.

Thoughout the twenties and thirties rent decontrol was sufficiently frequent to allow such property companies the hope of further decontrol and success in investments already undertaken. The truth of this statement can be seen from Table 24, which gives a history of rent-control limits on London. (The decontrolling provisions in other parts of the country followed the same pattern, but the rateable value limits were lower.)

This thumb-nail history of the legislation controlling rents shows how cleverly (but quite unwittingly) Parliament maintained investors' interest in dwelling-houses of the type which interest companies. During the ten years 1923 to 1933 all dwellings were automatically decontrolled on possession, and the hopes of landlords were kept alive by almost annual legislation. Every time the Acts came before Parliament for re-examination the landlords must have hoped that there would be a general reduction in the amount of control.

During the period 1923 to 1933 landlords who held property in the

*Table 24: Legislation controlling rents.*

| Year | | Control in London: rateable value not exceeding |
|------|---|---|
| 1915 | | £35 |
| 1920 | | £105 |
| 1923 | Decontrol by possession[1] | |
| 1925–7 | Legislation extending the period of 1923 Act | |
| 1927–33 | Annual legislation extending 1923 Act | |
| 1933 | Decontrol of houses over | £45 |
| | Decontrol by possession | £35 to £45 |
| | Decontrol on registration of possession | £20 to £35 |
| | No decontrol by possession unless decontrolled 1923 to 1933 and registered | £20 |
| 1938 | Decontrol of houses over | £35 |
| | No decontrol by possession of self-contained dwellings | £20 to £35 |
| 1939 | No decontrol | £100 |

expectation of future decontrol were in general able to get a competitive return on their capital as the Rent and Mortgage Interest (Restrictions) Act 1923 had permitted rent increases ranging from 15 to 40 per cent, according to the responsibilities undertaken by the landlord. These increases came when the 1919–22 inflation was over and coincided with a decrease in the earnings of manual workers. According to the Inland Revenue statistics, the earnings of manual workers fell from the 1920–1 aggregate level of £945 million to £520 million in 1921–2; and to £391 million in 1922–3. By 1933 the aggregate earnings had risen again to about £550 million. Thus, at a time when the aggregate incomes of manual workers fell over 40 per cent, rents rose by about 40 per cent and from 1923 to 1933 rents were probably controlled at about their market value. It is impossible to obtain any accurate information about the return obtained on rent-controlled property, but the following passage in *The Economist* does not suggest that the level of rents was below the market level.

. . . Investors have preferred to follow a waiting policy with regard to small houses, and investments have only changed hands where money was needed. There are buyers waiting to acquire this description of property on approximately an 8 per cent basis, but the difficulty would be for the seller to find anything like a similar return on his money in other directions.[2]

1. A letting was freed from rent control when the tenant left and the landlord regained possession of the dwelling.
2. *The Economist*, 24 January 1925.

During the six years 1933 to 1939 the level of rents may have gradually fallen behind the general level of incomes. This sets the general scene in which rent controls were operated in 1920 to 1939. It gives an average picture about which there were a great many variations. The average landlord must have retained hopes of decontrol, and he obtained a competitive return on his money. He also, probably, obtained the decontrol of about 3 per cent of his property by possession each year. In the course of ten years about one third of the properties will thus have been decontrolled. There are no statistics to support the assumed level of 3 per cent, but during the period 1950 to 1957 this was the average turnover rate in large London estates (a hundred or more tenancies) and it is unlikely to have been lower during a period of fairly heavy unemployment and labour mobility.

We have now to consider in general terms the effects of rent controls upon landlords whose property is greatly undervalued by rent control.

## Undervalued property

This is the sort of property in which companies are willing to invest so long as prospects of decontrol exist. The present value of the dwelling is far below its estimated future value, and investors able and willing to wait for their profits are likely to invest in this part of the market. Even during the years 1945 to 1955 there were enterprising directors of property companies willing to gamble on future profits from this type of residential property situated in or near town centres.

When the profits are at last obtainable, either through general decontrol or possession by vacancy, the profits can normally be most readily realized by sale, not necessarily of the freehold but of some leasehold interest. The general principle is to accept a lower than market return on capital for a few years and then to obtain at one time all the foregone return on the original capital. The alternative is to get a higher than market return on capital once the property is decontrolled, but this is an almost impossible thing to do. It is one thing for a businessman to be constrained by law to take a lower than average return on his capital, it is quite another thing for a businessman to persuade someone voluntarily to pay him a higher than average return on capital. Landlords who have been forced to accept lower than average returns by the control of rents may be content, on decontrol, with the current average return, but landlords who invest in controlled property after controls are introduced will only do so in the expectation of higher than average returns in the future, or capital gains.

The list of four alternative actions in Table 25 shows the possibilities which are open to landlords when decontrol is introduced. Each action has to be considered on the assumption that (1) the current market rate of interest is 6 per cent and (2) capital was invested in the property during the period of rent control and at the date of decontrol yielded a very low return of, say, 2 per cent.

*Table 25: Alternative actions open to a landlord after the decontrol of rent.*

|  |  | New yield on invested capital |
|---|---|---|
| Action 1: | Current valuation of property, say £1,000, new rent level (net of all expenses) £60 | 6% |
| Action 2: | Current valuation of property £1,000, sale of property at £1,000 investment of £1,000 in market to yield | 6% |
| or | Use of £1,000 to pay to shareholders high enough dividends to compensate them for long waiting period. | |
| Action 3: | Attempt to get tenant to pay yield of 10 per cent on £1,000 valuation. 4 per cent to compensate for loss over five years and 6 per cent to cover market rate | 10% |
| Action 4: | Sale of leasehold at £900 and ground rent of £12. | |
|  | Use £900 to compensate patient shareholders and induce leaseholder to pay a 12 per cent return on very small amount of capital | 12% |

Any one of the above actions might be favoured by the directors of a property company, but action 4 has most to recommend it. A willing purchaser can probably be found to pay 90 per cent of the property value, and if necessary to make his own mortgage arrangements. It is also very probable that a man can be found willing to pay a high rate of interest on the landlord's capital left in the land. It is one thing to pay 12 per cent on £100 and quite another to pay it on £1,000. So long as the ground rent does not exceed about £75 a willing tenant can be found to pay it. We are here, of course, speaking of desirable residential areas. It is in these districts where rent control quite clearly results in lower than market rents. If this analysis of market behaviour is correct the decontrol of rents is rather paradoxically the time at which we can expect the sale of dwellings to owner-occupiers rather than during the period of rent control.

### Areas where rent controls produce rents much nearer the market value

These areas are much more extensive than is normally imagined. Most people who think of rent controls do so in isolation from all other factors controlling the level of profits which can be obtained from dwellings. Below is a list of some of the other things which should be considered:

1. The general level of income.
2. The level of income of families willing to live in a particular street of dwellings.
3. All laws controlling property – public health laws in particular.
4. The activities of local authorities as suppliers of dwellings.
5. The price of mortgages.
6. The alternative places in which people are willing to live.
7. Cost of other things, particularly transport.
8. The subjective assessment of the quality of dwellings. This is something normally called 'taste' by economists and in property it covers the assessment of such things as the use of a garden. For instance, someone may be willing to pay 35s. per week for a dwelling without a garden, but not willing to pay 40s. Each individual family has different notions about these things and they are seldom very closely associated with the cost of providing the actual facility of bath, garden or other similar amenity.

Most of these things are relatively unimportant during a period of rent control because people think they are unimportant. As soon as rent controls are removed people know that they are very important and start actively taking them into consideration. If a tenant has been accustomed to paying a rent of £1 per week and his landlord asks him for a rent of 30s. a week, he is almost bound to make an assessment of the value he gets for his money. After such consideration he may come to the firm conclusion that his accommodation is very cheap at 30s. a week. If, however, the landlord has behaved 'rationally' he is not likely to reach this conclusion.

Suppose the landlord considers all the factors listed above and comes to the correct conclusion that his house is worth £2,000. He asks a rent which gives him the current return on property of 8 per cent (£160). Suppose a tenant views the house and comes to exactly the same conclusion as the landlord – the house is worth to the tenant £2,000.

Suppose, furthermore, that the tenant knows that he can get a mortgage of £1,600 from a building society on such a house. The mortgage re-payments over twenty years will be £140 and if the prospective tenant has not got the £400 deposit and has to rent property he will quite rightly regard his lack of capital as forcing him to pay a rate of interest of 12½ per cent on the £400 capital which he is in effect borrowing from the landlord. An account is given below of the transaction.

*Table 26: Account of purchase of a £2,000 house.*

| | |
|---|---:|
| Mortgage at 6 per cent on 20 years obtained on | £1,600 |
| Deposit of £400 made | 400 |
| Cost of house | £2,000 |
| Annual mortgage repayments (of which £96 is interest in 1st year and £44 is capital re-payment) | £140 |
| Tax relief at 7s. 9d. (earned income) on £96 | £29 |
| Total annual cost of dwelling in first year to owner-occupier | £111 |
| Rental cost | £160 |
| Mortgage cost | £111 |
| Difference | £49 |
| Interest which a tenant feels he has to pay on the £400 deposit which he does not possess and is therefore bound to rent a house instead of buying | 12½% |

NOTE: Incentive therefore exists for 'tenants' to save or borrow £400 at any interest less than 12½ per cent and become 'owner-occupiers'.

In other words if the tenant and the landlord are in agreement about the capital value of the house they are likely to be in disagreement over the rental value. The taxes imposed upon landlords will, of course, tend to accentuate still further this disagreement, because the landlord must try to get a post-tax rental which will give him as good a return as the post-tax income from any other source.

The difficulties of the landlord, and in particular his unfavourable tax position, is hidden by rent controls. It is only when rents are decontrolled that landlords unequivocally attempt to obtain a return on the current value of their houses. Under rent control they are forced to accept a return on the historic value and as they move from 'historic' to 'current' valuation they run into all the difficulties of 'exorbitant' rents, and accusations that they are 'sweating their properties'. Tenants who are unable to make the calculation given above none the less accuse their landlords of charging 'exorbitant' rents. If a landlord can at one and the same time avoid all social criticism and also obtain a higher return on his capital, he is likely to do this with great alacrity. Rent controls are, however, from his point of view, a devilish device by which he is prevented from doing so.

To understand the full impact of rent controls it is necessary to consider three aspects of value:

1. The historic value.
2. The current value.
3. The replacement cost.

## 1. The historic value

In J. B. Cullingworth's book *Housing in Transition*[1] some examples are given of the way landlords of Lancaster think of their investments. One of these examples describes a landlord who thought in terms of historic cost, and as it very vividly portrays this method of assessing returns on capital it is quoted below:

This landlord owned a pair of semi-detached houses, one of which he occupied himself. Both houses had been built and purchased by the present owner in 1938. The capital cost of the houses was £340 each. Following the Rent Act [1957] the rent was increased to 20s. (3s. 10d. below maximum). His net income was therefore £37. He maintained that he was getting a return of over 10 per cent on his original investment and that it was 'inflation-proof'.[2]

The contentment of this landlord is due to the fact that he thought in terms of the £340 which he paid for the investment in 1938. He was not charging the tenant the maximum rent presumably because he liked the tenant and was a very pleasant landlord. (The Lancaster local-authority four-bedroom houses were let at 29s. 6d. rent a week so the landlord could surely have got 23s. 10d. a week rent if he chose to ask for it.) If he had charged the full rent of 23s. 10d. his net return would have been increased by £10 a year to £47. At £47 net rent a year the value of the house as an investment would certainly not be £340, but some figure considerably higher.

1. J. B. Cullingworth, *Housing in Transition*, Heinemann Educational Books, 1963.
2. ibid., pp. 133–4.

Suppose that it is a generally accepted fact that this house will always be rent controlled and cannot ever be sold with vacant possession; then anyone buying the house must do so as an investment and they will argue that if they can 'buy' £5 a year by investing £100 on the Stock Exchange they will pay an equivalent price for the right to have £47 each year from this particular house. If the net rent had been £45, investors would be willing to pay £900 (nine times £100) for the right to receive the annual stream of income.

If the rate of interest on gilt-edged bonds is not 5 per cent but 6 per cent the investor will only be willing to give £880 for the right to obtain the annual sum of £47 (compared with £940 at 5 per cent for £47). Should the rate of interest fall to 4 per cent the investor will give £1,175. These figures have been quoted on the assumption that investors regard houses as identical to gilt-edged bonds. This is by no means true, but the principle is not altered by taking into account the differences between the two types of asset. If investors think houses are a risky investment and a much more troublesome investment than a bond, they will demand a higher return from the house. When the market rate on bonds is 6 per cent they will demand 7 per cent on dwellings, when it is 7 per cent they may demand 8 or 9 per cent on dwellings and so on.

Table 27 gives the capital needed to buy an annual income of £47 from a house (with a life of fifty years) without adjustment for taxes and with adjustment for taxes which have to be paid upon interest earned on a sinking-fund put aside to preserve the value of the asset. The figures

*Table 27: Capital value of annual income of £47.*

| Interest rate to be earned on capital | Capital value of £47 | |
|---|---|---|
| | *Without tax adjustment* | *With tax adjustment (Income tax at 7s. 9d. in pound)* |
| % | £ | £ |
| 5 | 780 | 704 |
| 6 | 669 | 612 |
| 7 | 586 | 542 |
| 8 | 521 | 486 |

show that there is no one 'current investment' price for this dwelling. However, the value lies somewhere between £480 and £780. At least we are able to say that it certainly is not £340 and that the relationship between £47 and £340 is only of great importance in that it makes the present owner of the property content. Indeed it makes him so content that he takes a lower rent and is well satisfied with £37.

## 2. *The current value*

In the above example we have moved from the 'historic' cost to the 'current investment cost' and we now move forward to the current price of an empty house. J. B. Cullingworth gives an example[1] of a landlord who was very discontented and thought in terms of the current price which he could get if only his houses were vacant.

A sixty-year-old office clerk whose property had come to him under his father's will twenty years ago, this landlord owned five houses which had been built in the thirties by his father for sale, but which owing to the saturation of the market had had to be let. Pre-1957 rents were 11s. 6d. [net] a week. Following the Rent Act they were increased to 25s. The houses had been kept in good condition so that they could be sold at a favourable price. No detailed records had been kept but the owner thought that on average he spent £15 a year per house on repairs, decoration and insurance. He considered £6 10s. a 'fair' allowance for management (which he undertook himself). On his reckoning therefore his position in regard to each house was:

| *Income* | | *Expenditure* | | | |
|---|---|---|---|---|---|
| | | | £ | s. | d. |
| Rent £65 | Repairs etc. | | 15 | 0 | 0 |
| | Management | | 6 | 10 | 0 |
| | | | £21 | 10s. | 0d. |

This gave a net income of £43 10s. Since the houses were, in the owner's view, worth £2,000, he maintained that he was getting only a little over 2 per cent on his investment, and that it was obviously much more profitable to sell.

This landlord was indulging in 'wishful thinking'.

In fact, he owns houses worth £500 to £600 each, and if he died and was assessed for Estate Duty his five houses would be valued at about £2,500. However, he has no wish to sell them at that price because at any time one of the houses may become vacant and he will then possess an entirely *different* commodity, which he can sell for perhaps £2,000. The 'commodity' he would then possess would be an unoccupied house. When one of the houses becomes vacant the landlord has two economic commodities to sell – both 'space' and 'shelter', but while the houses remain occupied and rent controlled he has only one thing to sell – a rental income. So long as this landlord concentrates upon the prospects of eventually getting £2,000 for each house he will hold on to the asset and remain a 'landlord'.

1. op. cit., p. 133.

Suppose, however, that something happens to convince the landlord that all rents were going to be decontrolled in two to five years' time. If he thinks he will continue to get a controlled rent of about £40 a year for three years and then any rent he likes, say £160, he will calculate the present-day value of the house in the following way:

| | |
|---|---|
| Rent value after decontrol | £160 |
| Capital value at 6 per cent | £2,667 |
| Existing rent | £40 |
| Capital value at 6 per cent | £667 |

Here the 'hardcore' of the rental value is £40, and if decontrol in three years' time is a certainty, the 'marginal income' of the rental value is £120. The capital value of the marginal income in perpetuity is £2,000. If, however, there was no certainty of decontrol, the risks of gambling on the political decision to decontrol will lower the capital value of the 'marginal income' and it may drop back to zero. This is in effect the position described in the first example. We assumed there that rent control would last for fifty years and the value of the house depended entirely upon the current rent.

The price actually paid for any house will depend upon both factors:

(a) present rent;
(b) expected future rent based upon a valuation of the house if it could be freely let in the market.

As an assessment of the second factor depends largely upon the guesses made by individuals about future political behaviour the price paid for houses tends to fluctuate much more than it would in a completely free market. The level of the 'present rent' is the most important element and, as we have seen, it tends to keep down the capital value of houses.

Sales to 'sitting tenants' are not uncommon and are made by land-lords who reckon that half a loaf today is better than a doubtful possibility of cake tomorrow. However, sales to sitting tenants are seldom very profitable, as the following account shows:

### Account

| | |
|---|---|
| Rent income from a controlled house | £47 |
| Capital value as an investment (see example on page 121) | £500 to £600 |
| Maximum capital value of house sold to sitting tenant who pays income tax at 7s. 9d. in pound of earned income | £750 |

This example is worked out on the basis that a sitting tenant can get a 100 per cent mortgage at 6 per cent repayable over twenty-five years and that his annual outgoings must be kept to £47. If he bought the house for £750 he would pay almost £59 a year in mortgage repayments and in the first year he would get tax relief of about £13 5s., bringing the total cost of the mortgage down to about £47 in the first year. If the tenant can be persuaded to think that decontrol is going to be introduced in three or four years' time he may, of course, be persuaded to pay more if the value of decontrolled residential property is steadily rising. However, it seems that just as many landlords think of the value of their house in terms of vacant possession, so most tenants think of the value of houses in terms of rent controls lasting for ever.

From this discussion it seems very clear that while rent controls last landlords cannot escape from their predicament. The difference between current investment price and vacant possession price is too large and the landlord is forced to take the best profit he can from the house and to wait with as much patience as possible for the day when he can stop being a landlord.

### Profits obtained from rent-controlled property

As with almost all other aspects of British housing, we have no statistics upon which we can make really reliable estimates of the net income obtained from rented accommodation. Much of this book has stressed the tax burden imposed upon landlords and the reader may by now feel that the landlords have been very ill-treated during the last fifty years. However, this conclusion is valid only with respect to the imposition of taxes upon his capital asset. It is by no means certain that landlords have been denied opportunities to make a satisfactory return from rent-controlled property.

We have already seen that 'return' on capital is related to the way in which the capital is valued. If rent-controlled property is valued with reference to current owner-occupation values, then obviously the measured return is very low, but if it is measured against the current investment value it can be high or low – everything depends upon the rate of interest selected. It also depends upon the amount of money invested.

Normally the 'return on capital' tends to fall as the amount of capital involved rises. For instance, a 5 per cent return on £2,000,000 is often thought to yield an adequate income, but a 5 per cent return on £1,000 is a very inadequate income. A man with only £1,000 may possibly risk it in some enterprise which he hopes will yield 12½ per cent or an even higher rate of return. These differential rates of interest would be removed if everyone behaved 'rationally' and institutions and people with large capital assets tried to 'maximize their profits'.

In residential property the differential rates are found to operate in a direction opposite to that normally found. Instead of the large companies being the ones which obtain a fairly small return and the small individual being the one who takes risks and obtains a higher return, the position is reversed. A large property company specializing in rent-controlled property may manage to obtain a gross return of 16 per cent on the purchase of the property, while an individual landlord may only obtain a gross return of about 8 per cent or even less.

This difference is not due to the fact that the large companies do not do repairs or that they charge illegally high rents. On the contrary, a property company is usually just as good as and often much better than a private individual in carrying out repairs. The reason for the higher profits obtained by property companies is primarily related to the size of their holdings. If a large estate (more than a hundred houses) comes on to the market for sale in one block, only a fairly large company has the financial resources to bid for it. Each of the companies will have a definite upper figure which they are prepared to pay for the property. This figure was determined before 1954 by the total rent roll. If the total net rents were £10,000 a year and the company wanted a 10 per cent gross return on the property, the maximum price the directors would be willing to pay would be £100,000.

In view of the political risks of putting money in ordinary rent-controlled property, the rate of return demanded was often above 10 per cent and in 1950 to 1955 companies could buy such property on eight or even six years' purchase. If the estates had been broken up and each house sold separately the original owner would have obtained a higher total price for his property. As, however, he would then have been taxed as a 'dealer' in property, the net cash which the owner retained would probably have been less than if he sold it as a capital asset at one auction. This particular tax provision operates to frustrate the demand of potential owner-occupiers and has restricted the competition for large residential estates.

Only a relatively small number of companies are interested in residential property as an investment, and if each of them operates on a minimum gross return of 10 to $12\frac{1}{2}$ per cent, this becomes the rate of return on property of this type. Individual houses which are let at controlled rents do sometimes come on the market, but companies are not normally interested in an isolated house because of the extremely

9

large management costs and the low possibilities of development. These houses are therefore bought by other individuals. Some are bought as an investment but most appear to be bought in the hope of obtaining vacant possession in the foreseeable future. The price which such people are willing to pay depends upon a multitude of factors including the age of tenants. In large cities where houses are in multiple occupation, houses are sometimes bought partly as an investment and partly as a home for the owner.

### Level of rents and cost of repairs

In 1962 a survey of housing conditions in England was carried out by the Rowntree Trust Housing Study Team[1] as part of a long-term study of housing in England and the effects of housing policy since 1957. The survey covered 3,231 private households in England which had been selected by sampling techniques from the valuation lists. From this survey the information about net rents in Table 28 was obtained.

*Table 28: Net annual rent paid for unfurnished accommodation rented from a private landlord in 1962.[2]*

| Net annual rent | England Percentage of rents falling within range | |
|---|---|---|
| | | Cumulative total |
| Less than £10 | 2 | 2 |
| £10 to £20 | 7 | 9 |
| £20 to £30 | 13 | 22 |
| £30 to £40 | 17 | 39 |
| £40 to £50 | 13 | 52 |
| £50 to £60 | 10 | 62 |
| £60 to £70 | 7 | 69 |
| £70 to £80 | 5 | 74 |
| £80 to £90 | 4 | 78 |
| £90 to £100 | 3 | 81 |
| £100 to £200 | 7 | 88 |
| £200 to £300 | 2 | 90 |
| £300 and over | negligible | |
| Not known | 7 | 97 |
| Other (negligible, zero rent etc). | 3 | 100 |

1. For a full account of this research, see J. B. Cullingworth, *English Housing Trends*, Occasional Papers on Social Administration No. 13, Bell, 1965.
2. Research done by the Rowntree Trust Housing Study, fully reported in ibid.

In Chapter 5 the Inland Revenue statistics of Schedule A payments by owner-occupiers were quoted to show the cost of repairs carried out by owner-occupiers. The Schedule A statutory allowance for repairs was apparently sufficiently high to allow 90 per cent of all owner-occupiers to maintain their houses without making any additional claim for tax relief in respect of repair costs in excess of the Schedule A allowance. As there are no other available statistics it seems reasonable to assume that private landlords spent as much on repairs as the 90 per cent of owner-occupiers who were satisfied with their Schedule A allowance.

The average Schedule A allowance for owner-occupiers with incomes ranging from £180 to £1,000 was £5 to £6 per annum. As repair costs rose considerably from 1959 to 1962, the figure of £6 might be doubled to give some indication of the average cost of repairing a house in 1962.[1]

Table 29 gives net rent paid by ranges, and if we take the centre of each range and subtract £12 for repairs and £6 for management costs we shall get some approximation to the extent to which rents were covering the costs of management in 1962.[2]

*Table 29: Net rents; repairs and management; net income.*

| Rent | Repairs and management | Net income | Percentage of tenants |
|---|---|---|---|
| Less than £10 | £18 | $\left.\begin{array}{c} - 8 \\ - 3 \end{array}\right\}$ | 9 |
| £15 | £18 | | |
| £25 | £18 | $\left.\begin{array}{c} 7 \\ 17 \end{array}\right\}$ | 30 |
| £35 | £18 | | |
| £45 | £18 | $\left.\begin{array}{c} 27 \\ 37 \end{array}\right\}$ | 23 |
| £55 | £18 | | |
| £65 | £18 | $\left.\begin{array}{c} 47 \\ 57 \end{array}\right\}$ | 12 |
| £75 | £18 | | |
| £85 | £18 | $\left.\begin{array}{c} 67 \\ 77 \end{array}\right\}$ | 7 |
| £95 | £18 | | |

1. Some factual information on the cost of repairs is given in Cullingworth, op. cit., pp. 124–38 (particularly p. 135).

2. By late 1965 the figure of £18 should be raised to at least £25 to cover repair and management costs. As controlled rents had remained constant from 1957 to 1965, many more houses must have become totally unprofitable by 1965.

From Table 29 there seems little doubt that 9 per cent of all rented property is 'totally unprofitable' and a further 30 per cent is of very doubtful profitability. However, the totally unprofitable houses represent only 2·9 per cent of the total houses in the country and the ones of doubtful profitability represent only 9·7 per cent of the total stock. Table 30 shows these magnitudes a little more clearly.

*Table 30: Houses and flats by tenure, 1962, in England.*[1]

|  | Percentage of total stock |
|---|---|
| Owner-occupiers | 44 |
| Tenants | 56 |
|    of which local-authority tenants 22% | |
|        Private landlords' tenants 32% (unfurnished) | |
|        Private landlords' tenants  2% (furnished) | |
| 9% of private landlord's property is unprofitable; 9% of 32%=2·9% | |
| 30% of private landlord's property is of doubtful profitability  30% of 32%=9·7% | |
| *Conclusion:* 2·9% of the total stock is unprofitable      9·7% is of doubtful profitability | |

The fact that nearly 3 per cent of the total stock of dwellings show losses should neither surprise nor alarm anyone. Everything wears out in the end and an object is clearly shown to be worn out when the repair costs exceed annual revenue. Whether we have rent controls or not, each year some of the stock of houses must be finally worn out and should be replaced. Three per cent is a very low figure if it is considered in relation to the deplorable condition of some of the houses in British cities.

It is worth noting that the figures quoted above relate to the whole of England. If we examine the figures for the 'conurbations' of London, Birmingham, south-east Lancashire, Merseyside, West Yorkshire and Tyneside we find that the percentage of totally unprofitable houses is only 1·6 and those at the margin represent only 4·4 per cent of the total stock.

## 3. Replacement cost

What has been said above has been written on the assumption that privately-let accommodation is a dying industry and that no landlord

1. Material from the Rowntree Trust Housing Study.

manages his estate on the assumption that he will one day pull down the old houses and rebuild to let. If rebuilding is introduced into the argument, then it becomes abundantly clear that rents are much too low to induce any landlord to rebuild. With the very high prevailing levels of tax, rents would have to be so high to induce rebuilding that all tenants would flee to the owner-occupied or local-authority sector of the market. The best that a private landlord can now hope for is sufficient money to cover all the costs of repair and management and a return on the price which he paid for the property.

In this chapter we have seen that the landlord has been held by rent controls in a vice. One side of the vice is the historic price paid for the dwelling. On this historic-price basis a return on capital is made – sometimes a very high return, sometimes a very low return, but a return of some sort or another. The other side of the vice has been the current vacant-house price. If the landlord is to get that price he must wait. The laws controlling rents give him no alternative but to wait and manage his property as economically as he can while he is waiting. As soon as rent controls are lifted he moves out of the business of letting accommodation on weekly rents, unless his property is in the centre of a town and he can obtain a pure rent for the land upon which the house stands. In places like London rents are not related to the cost of building, repairing and managing houses, but to the cost of land. The cost of land is, of course, determined wholly by its scarcity.

## Conclusions

This discussion of rent controls has concentrated upon the difficulties which arise when decontrol is introduced. If all the financial organizations had remained exactly the same between 1915, when rents were first controlled, and 1957, when a large measure of decontrol was introduced, the movement from a controlled to an uncontrolled market would not have been so difficult. We have seen, however, that there were many very substantial economic changes between 1915 and 1957 which have made the private landlord's economic position *vis-à-vis* the owner-occupier and the local-authority landlord quite unprofitable.

The three main developments were not directly caused by rent controls. The increase in building-society funds cannot be explained by rent controls, neither can the great increase in taxation which was the result of two wars and a vast extension of government activity. Some people may argue that the increase in local-authority housing has been partly caused by the decreased supply of privately rented accommodation. There may be some truth in this, but it would be equally plausible to argue that the provision of houses by the 'state' is just one of many twentieth-century social developments. The result of a concern for the 'poor' and the needs of public health rather than of an artificially created shortage of dwellings to rent.

If there had been no rent controls, the general course of economic and commercial development of the country would probably have led to the introduction of large company landlords drawing their capital from the Stock Exchange by the issue of shares. Such a development would, however, have been blighted by the heavy taxation which falls upon the capital assets of property companies. If the companies had to use any financial arrangement which enforced repayment of loans, the levels of taxation over the past thirty years would have made it necessary for such companies to collect in rents a larger amount than an owner-occupier would have had to pay to a building society each year. For these reasons, and not because of rent controls, it does not seem economically possible that even large companies could have survived the twentieth century unless they turned from letting houses to the buying and selling of property either on lease or freehold.

It is only in the centre of towns that the private landlord still has an economic opportunity to compete successfully against the building societies. He is able to do this when there is no rent control by charging a rent for his property which fully reflects the scarcity of land in densely populated areas. As building societies are basically unwilling to compete with the landlord in this field, the landlord has only to contend with high taxation and local authorities. The high levels of taxation do not worry such landlords very much (if indeed at all) because the rising value of land puts them into the position of the nineteenth-century landlord who did not need to worry about repaying a loan. A mortgage can always be obtained on the land value of property in good residential neighbourhoods such as Chelsea or Kensington. The landlord does not, therefore, need to 'depreciate' his buildings and accumulate a fund to repay a mortgage given on the value of buildings.

Building societies do not seriously compete with the landlord in these very good residential districts because they must have their mortgages repaid and therefore insist that the money they lend bears some relationship to the purchaser's income. Usually they are willing to lend up to three times the annual income of the borrower. This fixes the capital value of the house in terms of current incomes, but few landlords would sell such a valuable asset unless they obtained a capital sum which reflected the higher incomes expected to prevail in three to ten years' time. Thus even if people want to become owner-occupiers in places like central London, they cannot easily do so because there are insufficient financial institutions to finance the purchase by individuals of very expensive land.

Local authorities are a greater source of concern to urban landlords because they may compulsorily purchase their land. For this and other non-economic reasons few 'reputable' property companies buy houses which would commonly be designated 'slum property'. In this context 'reputable' means a company which expects to remain in business for at least another twenty years and has a slightly paternalistic attitude to its tenants. Such companies are very often some of the best landlords and work upon the principle that an 8 per cent return and contented tenants is a financially sounder business proposition than a 12½ per cent return and an extremely discontented group of tenants who form themselves into aggressive tenants' associations. Property companies of this type are not concerned with high short-run profits, they are concerned for their shareholders long-term interests and in the truest sense they are not dealers, but 'investors' in property.

The companies cannot, however, operate in isolation from the main stream of economic events, and to attract and retain capital they are having to diversify their property holdings and are shifting towards investment in commercial buildings. There are only three major types of investor in shops and offices: property companies, insurance companies, and the manufacturing and retailing firms who own and occupy the premises. These three investors are, from the economic point of view, fairly evenly matched. Thus each one has an equal opportunity to make profits (and losses). It is not therefore surprising to find property companies taking their expertise in property development and management out of the field of residential property and into the commercial sector.

These facts account for the apparent paradox that the decontrol of rents leads not to the supply of more rented accommodation in the U.K. but to less. If, when decontrols were introduced in 1957, the Government had also introduced a measure of tax reform so that landlords could depreciate their buildings, it is possible that the shift to owner-occupation would have been delayed for another twenty years. The opportunity was, however, lost, and we now have the unfortunate combination of high rents in towns, where owner-occupation is restricted by a lack of financial arrangement for its extension, with a final loss of rental accommodation in the suburbs, where landlords cannot compete with building-society or local-authority mortgage arrangements.

An attempt has been made to discuss these topics from the economic position of the landlord, but it should not be forgotten that the tenant of the private landlord suffers doubly from these developments. First he is left out of all the subsidy arrangements, and secondly the tenant of a private landlord living in 'uncontrolled' property has permanently to pay the current value of the property he occupies. With rising money incomes the owner-occupier and the local-authority tenant benefit from the reduced real burden of the capital repayment of loans incurred in a period of lower prices. Once rent controls are removed and security of tenure is taken away from the private landlord's tenant, the rent charged to the tenant is constantly reassessed to take into account the 'current' level of incomes.

An example of the way in which this works may help the reader to grasp the significance of this to a tenant of uncontrolled property.

*Example*: A street of a hundred houses, one of which becomes vacant and is sold for £3,000.

The price of £3,000 is paid because there are several people wanting this house and only one is available. If all the 100 houses became vacant simultaneously the price per house might well fall to £1,500 or £2,000. The £3,000 actually paid is of course a reflection of the 'shortage' of dwellings. However, the sale of the one house sets the value on all the other houses because if any of them became vacant it could also be sold for £3,000. Thus a 'rational' landlord will argue that he can either sell his house for £3,000 and invest this money to get the current market return of say 6 per cent, or he can leave his capital in the house and get the same return from that source. If he chooses to leave it in the house he must charge a net rent of £180.

Now suppose that in a year another house is sold and because of inflation and a continuing housing shortage it fetches £4,000. The landlord is faced with exactly the same choice as before and if he again decides to leave the capital in the house he must now get a return of £240 if the rate of interest is still 6 per cent.

From the above example it is clear that inflation without rent controls is another reason for tenants to shift to the owner-occupied section of the housing market. Thus to lift rent controls in a period of inflation is to invite a rapid escape from rental property, which sets up a cycle of rising prices. As tenants realize that rents rise with each market revaluation of the property, they realize that 'if only they had bought last year' they would not now have to pay the current value of their property but last year's lower value. Therefore they make a greater effort to buy. Thus those who wish to buy increase in number and force the selling price of houses still higher. Since all houses are valued with reference to the few which are actually sold, rents rise almost as rapidly as the capital value of houses for sale. Once this process has been started it is very difficult to stop because the price of all accommodation is fixed with reference to the artificially enhanced price of the few dwellings which actually come upon the market.

In Chapter 10 some suggestions will be made for a system of rent controls which gives landlords a 'fair' return on their invested capital while at the same time giving to tenants some security and constancy in the level of rent which they pay. The suggestions which will be made are, however, a mere palliative and are only intended to make it easier for both landlords and tenants during the final period of transition from nineteenth-century housing finance to the twentieth-century forms, which must finally lead to 90 per cent of property being either owner-occupied or owned by landlords who operate on a non-commercial basis.

# CHAPTER 9

# *Incomes and Prices*

It has already been seen that the most important factor in housing economics is the capital price of the house and the financial arrangements made for borrowing and taxing this capital. The money may be borrowed directly from a lender or indirectly through a landlord who invests his capital in houses. The amount of capital needed can best be measured in terms of the average annual income of heads of households. By relating the price of a house to the average income of men and/or families, we can convert the cost of housing into the real national cost of supplying accommodation.

In Great Britain the average price of a new house is approximately 2·7 times the average annual earnings of male workers.[1] In other European countries, the ratio is somewhat higher, but direct comparisons are impossible because of the varying standards of house building. A comparison of different countries does, however, show conclusively that the cost of building a house always necessitates some borrowing by the average skilled and unskilled workers of the country. The ratio of 2·7 for the United Kingdom is the lowest in Europe and it arises because of the efficiency with which we build small houses and the fact that most of our houses are constructed in traditional style and material. In the building of flats, we are somewhat less efficient than builders in other European countries.[2]

The relationship of house prices to income is not accidental. The variations between one country and another may be due to the accident of history and geography, but for any one country, the long-term ratio of house prices to income is determined by the financial institutions available to finance the houses as well as by social custom. In some countries, people are for one reason or another unwilling to pay a high proportion of their income for housing. In other countries, a high level

1. *Financing of Housing in Europe*, U.N. Economic Commission for Europe, Geneva, 1958, pp. 2 and 3, and 40–1.

2. *Financing of Housing in Europe: Cost Repetition Maintenance Related to Aspects of Building Prices*, U.N. Economic Commission for Europe, Geneva, 1963.

of rent or mortgage repayments is acceptable. Some of the variation must be due to historic circumstances, perhaps first developed many hundreds of years ago when money incomes were first introduced into city life. As the use of money spread, city families became accustomed to devoting a certain amount of their income to rent. Gradually, financial institutions developed to meet the particular customs of the country.

Unfortunately, there are very few statistics on the price of houses in the U.K. prior to 1919, but the scattered information which is available suggests that, during the eighteenth and nineteenth centuries, the price of a small family house was about three times the annual wage-level of the families for whom the house was intended. The price paid for building a house will, of course, determine the quality of the house and the standard of housing which the nation attains. In the U.K. there has been a certain reluctance to invest in residential property and Englishmen are not normally willing to pay more than 20 to 25 per cent of their income in rent or mortgage repayment. As the annual payments on a house determine the capital value of the house, these levels of rent will determine the standard of housing which generally prevails. On the Continent, families are equally unwilling to pay a high proportion of their income in rent, but they seem to insist on a higher standard of equipment in their houses and this they obtain at the expense of space.

In Britain, space is given a very high ranking in consumer preferences, whereas central heating and modern plumbing is given a relatively low ranking. For these reasons, we cannot compare the capital cost of building in different countries without taking into account other costs which are involved in utilizing the accommodation. The Englishman must, for instance, spend a good deal of money in heating his spacious but rather draughty house and he has also to spend a considerable amount of time and money in travelling from his house to his work. On the Continent, there appears to be more expenditure on the structure of the house and the equipment which is built into it, and less expenditure on travel and heating.

From 1920, statistics are available on the average price of houses built by local authorities in England and Wales. These statistics of building costs can be related to the series of Ministry of Labour statistics of weekly wages and earnings. In relating these two series of statistics, we are unfortunately able to obtain only a rough measure of the relationship between the cost of building and average earnings, because the Ministry of Labour statistics relate to weekly wage-levels and in order to arrive at an annual income the weekly wages have to be multiplied by fifty-two. However, we know that during the period

1920–39 average annual wages were normally considerably less than the average weekly wages multiplied by fifty-two. The difference arose because of unemployment, sickness, or short-time working and the estimated annual statistic of wages must therefore be used with caution.

From these statistics[1] we find that a local-authority house built in 1925 cost £510, which was 2·3 times the wage of a skilled craftsman and 3 times a labourer's wage. If we add £70 to the building cost to cover the price of land and roads, the price of a house with land was 2·7 times the skilled wage and 3·5 times the unskilled wage.[2] Prices fell between 1925 and 1931 and reduced the ratios to 1·9 and 2·6 for the building alone and 2·3 and 3 for both the land and the building. From about 1931–9, building prices and wages rose slightly (from an average 1931 price for a house of £404 to the 1939 price of £438), but the ratios remained fairly constant.

For the period 1951–63 there are no statistics of the average purchase price of a local-authority house (i.e. land plus building). However, there are statistics of the average tender price of a three-bedroom house built by local authorities in England and Wales. These show that the average cost has fallen from about 3 times the average annual *earnings* in 1951 to about 2·2 times the average earnings in 1962. The addition of land and other costs would perhaps raise the average 1962 level to 2·3 times the skilled worker's earnings and 3 times the unskilled, but in large cities the addition of the land costs would greatly raise the ratio of house purchase price to annual income.

Instead of using Ministry of Labour statistics, we could use the income-tax statistics published by the Inland Revenue. These statistics have to be used with even greater caution than those of the Ministry of Labour as many people who pay income tax do not want houses and therefore their incomes are irrelevant in discussing the housing problem. *Per contra*, many people who want houses do not pay tax and are therefore excluded from the Inland Revenue statistics. The unemployed, widows and old-age pensioners are, for instance, excluded. Teenage employees are included but they do not normally want a house until they are married. Nevertheless the figures can be used to give some idea of the magnitude of the housing problem for a large number of families.

From the Inland Revenue 105th Report[3] we find that the median income of people living and working in the County of London in 1959–60

1. *Ministry of Labour Gazette*, 1919–39.
2. See *Housing and Housing Subsidies Since the End of the First World War*, Statistical Memorandum No. 29, House of Commons Library, 13 December 1955.
3. Report of Commissioners of H.M. Inland Revenue, H.M.S.O., January 1963, Cmnd 1906, Table 108.

was £659. That is to say 50 per cent of the individuals (a husband and wife being counted as one individual) had more than £659 in the tax year 1959–60 and 50 per cent had less. During the same year the Co-operative Permanent Building Society reported[1] that the average price of an *existing* house in London was £2,324. This price was 3·5 times the median income. The average price of the *new* houses in London which the Co-operative Permanent Building Society mortgaged was £3,025, or 4·59 times the median income. In Scotland where the median income was lower (£564) the average price of a new house was also lower (£2,607), but the relationship between the median income and the price of a new house was almost the same: 4·65 compared with the London level of 4·59. However, in Scotland the price of existing houses was substantially lower, being only 2·87 times the median income as compared with the London level of 3·53.

The price of a house can also be examined in the light of the Inland Revenue statistics of Schedule E incomes.[2] Schedule E incomes are those in which the principal source of income is from employment so that the statistics reflect the average income of most working men and women. In 1959–60, the median Schedule E income of men was £640 and, taking the average price of a new house as £2,482,[2] the ratio of house to income was 3·9. Women were earning considerably less and only 6·4 per cent of all the women paying Schedule E tax earned £640 or more in 1959.

Existing houses are normally a great deal cheaper than new houses and in 1959–60 borrowers from the Co-operative Permanent Building Society paid an average price of £1,673 for the old houses which they bought. This price is about 2·55 times the median Schedule E income of £640. The relationship between the price of new and existing houses depends almost entirely upon the demand for accommodation, and when there is a great shortage of houses an old house may sell for almost the same price as a new house. This is particularly true when the old houses are situated in highly desirable residential areas. The effects of demand can be seen in Table 31, which gives the percentage by which the price of a new house exceeded that of an existing house in the years 1959–63.

In London, where the pressure of demand upon the existing housing stock is greatest, there is the smallest difference between the price of new and old houses. The general way in which the prices narrowed

1. *Co-operative Permanent Building Society Occasional Bulletin.*

2. Report of Commissioners of H.M. Inland Revenue, H.M.S.O., January 1962, Cmnd 1958, Table 67.

between 1959 and 1964 is a reflection of the removal of rent controls, the easing of credit and the increased flow of funds to building societies and insurance companies. Up to 1958, the building societies had never advanced more than £400 million on mortgage in one year; in 1959 they advanced more than £500 million and by 1963 the amount had risen to £850 million. As the building of new houses did not increase proportionately to meet the forces which were changing the effective demand for houses, the price of old houses was bid up relative to the price of new houses.

*Table 31: Percentages by which the price of a new house exceeded the price of an existing house (last quarter of each year).*[1]

|               | 1959 | 1960 | 1961 | 1962 | 1963 | 1964 |
|---------------|------|------|------|------|------|------|
| London        | 30   | 23   | 5·6  | 5·7  | 0·3  | 2·6  |
| Southern      | 48   | 40   | 18   | 20   | 1·2  | 0·6  |
| Western       | 51   | 54   | 44   | 30   | 12·3 | 3·1  |
| Midland       | 54   | 56   | 37   | 32   | 11·4 | 5·5  |
| Eastern       | 39   | 27   | 19   | 29   | 13·8 | 8·1  |
| North-western | 86   | 75   | 54   | 62   | 18·1 | 15·1 |
| North-eastern | 60   | 53   | 40   | 47   | 16·8 | 19.5 |
| Scotland      | 61   | 48   | 46   | 42   | 22·6 | 10·9 |

The statistics of house prices have been taken from the Co-operative Permanent Building Society, but the figures for another society (Leek and Moorlands Building Society) confirm the narrow difference which existed between the price of the new and existing houses which they mortgaged at the beginning of 1963. The average prices were: new houses £3,007, existing houses £2,844. These average figures relate to houses situated in many different parts of the country and to houses of different ages and sizes, so care is needed in interpreting the statistics.

From the figures of incomes and house prices, it is clear that 50 per cent of families are likely to have a 'housing problem' if the only way in which they can obtain accommodation is by bidding for it in a free market. In Table 2 in Chapter 3 the proportion of income spent on servicing a mortgage was given, and from this table it seems that three times the annual income is about the maximum amount at present interest rates which a family can borrow if not more than 20 to 24 per cent of the owner's income is to be spent on purchasing accommodation.

1. *Co-operative Permanent Building Society Occasional Bulletins*, 1959–63.

For the family who must rent accommodation because they cannot afford to buy it, the maximum capital price of house and land can also be stated as a multiple of income. If a private landlord must have a 7 per cent minimum return (and in view of his tax position and the fact that he borrows at 6 per cent this is much below the minimum commercial return), the maximum capital price of a dwelling is three times the income of the tenant if the net rent is not to exceed 20 per cent of the tenant's income. The problems of the poorer than average tenants in London, where old houses were equal to 4·5 times the median income in 1959–60, can thus be imagined. Those who obtained less than the median income or had particularly large families were clearly in the grave economic position of having to pay 40 to 50 per cent of their income in rent even if landlords only charged a rent which yielded a 7 per cent gross pre-tax return on capital.

*Building costs and land prices*

The reason why dwellings are so expensive relative to income is due partly to the real costs of building a house, including the costs of producing the materials, and partly to the cost of land. When the cost of building is equivalent to three times the annual wage of an unskilled man, the addition of land will tend to make it impossible for unskilled workers to pay an economic rent for new houses. These families can, however, normally afford to pay an economic rent for an old house. Skilled workers are in a better position, but the price of land can obstruct the economic effort of the skilled worker to obtain a new dwelling.

Land prices rise to 'ration' land according to the income of different families. If, as in London, there is great pressure for the available land, skilled workers are, like unskilled workers, priced out of the market. However, in most districts the skilled worker's income is above the average income and the income levels of skilled workers constitutes one of the important factors in determining the overall level of rents and house prices. Normally the market price of a house is not above the level which skilled workers can afford to pay, provided they have an assured regular income and a family of average size.

The relationship between a worker's annual income and the cost of building a house can, of course, be varied by technical increases in productivity and by variations in the levels of profit obtained by the building firm. In the long run, however, the level of profits in Great Britain is determined by the builders' necessity to sell houses to families who are only able and willing to buy or rent houses which cost about three times their annual income level.

Increased productivity through technological advances does not necessarily lead to a lowering of the total cost of building. There are three objectives of technical advance:

1. Increased speed of production.
2. Changes in the types of dwelling produced, e.g. the production of tall blocks of flats.
3. Lowering costs of production by using more capital and less labour during periods of rising labour costs.

The first two types of technical advance do not necessarily lead to cheaper costs and, in fact, often lead to an increase because the aim of the technical improvements is not to lower costs but to meet some other economic need, such as an urgent social need for more houses, or to meet the economic necessity to economize in the use of land. If the primary objective is not to reduce costs, but to achieve a greater speed of production, any incidental savings in cost are often used to increase the amenities of the estates. If, for instance, £200 can be saved on each house or flat built, the £200 'saved' on the dwelling may be used to cover the cost of garages or an improved play-area for children. This tendency seems fairly widespread, and as both garages and improved children's play-spaces are much needed, there seems little hope of obtaining a lowering in building costs in the near future through technical changes introduced to increase the speed of production or to make fuller use of the limited amount of land available by building tall blocks of flats.

Technological changes introduced quite specifically to lower costs have so far been relatively unsuccessful in Britain. In other countries which have managed to introduce cost-saving devices it seems to have been partly at the expense of quality. The difficulty of achieving real cost savings stems from the fact that, as the amount of labour used to build houses falls, the amount of capital used is greatly increased. Because interest rates have not been low in the post-war period the annual cost of capital equipment is very high, and if some of it is idle during the building operation, the costs of the capital equipment will equal or even exceed the costs of labour which it displaces. This is particularly likely to happen when the shift to a capital intensive building technique has been made in order to increase the speed of production.

Some of the capital costs could be reduced by making full use of each piece of capital and programming all work on site so that the machinery arrived when it was needed and was transferred to another site as soon as it had been used. This, however, calls for more management skill than is normally available in building firms or the direct labour departments of local authorities. However, a very intensive effort to lower costs by detailed forward planning and the formation of groups of local authorities which would have sufficient aggregate demand to make full use of all capital equipment may, eventually, lower the cost of building. It is, however, probably 'wishful thinking' to expect this to occur in the immediate future.

## The price of land

The cost of land is much more variable than the cost of building and is subject to fluctuation with the changing distribution and level of incomes. While the cost of building may remain constant over a long period of years, the price paid for land can change with great rapidity with changes in fashion. Normally, in every city, there is a fashionable area; and another area occupied by artists, intellectuals and actors, who may not have very high incomes but are prepared to live a bohemian life and do not demand very high standards of housing. Then there are other areas in which the majority of people are either of the middle-income group or of the lower-income wage-earning group. Sometimes, a change of fashion can occur and one or other of these groups will move into an area not previously occupied by this particular income group. When this occurs, the price of land may change very rapidly indeed. If it is a wealthier income group occupying an area previously occupied by weekly wage-earners, the price of land can double or treble in a year or two. On the other hand, if an area once fashionable loses its status as a desirable residential neighbourhood, the price of land will fall.

Very little is known about the price paid for land, partly because the statistics are not collected and published in the U.K., and partly because, even if they were published, land changes hands relatively rarely and it would be difficult to disentangle inflationary increases from increases due to a change in the desirability of a residential area. During the period 1957–64, the price of land in many parts of the country has risen considerably owing to the decontrol of rents. Some of this increase in price has been due to the general inflation which has occurred between 1939–64. But some of the increase in land prices has been due to the operation of rent controls since 1915.

When rent control was first introduced, the price of land on which rent-controlled houses were situated must have fallen to some extent relative to land that was free from all government restriction. This is

10

because the price paid for land is a direct reflection of the amount of income which can be obtained from the land. If, by rent control, the Government prevents rental income from rising when the general level of income rises, the price of land will be as effectively controlled as if the Government had imposed controls directly upon the land. Thus, when rents were decontrolled in 1957, the owners of some houses, which had been rent controlled since 1915, were able for the first time in forty years to obtain a capital sum for the land, which represented the rental which would be paid for the land in a free market. In places like Westminster and Chelsea, where some small lettings had been continually controlled since 1915, the value of the property rose on decontrol by as much as 500 to 600 per cent. But in areas just a little farther from the centre of London, the decontrol of rents raised the value of the land by very much less. It is difficult to be at all precise in making an estimate of the extent to which the decontrol of rents raised the general level of land prices, but it would not be surprising if the general level of increase was about 100 per cent.

In considering the price of land, it is of course important to remember that, as the price rises, its density of use is also increased, so that the level of land-cost per dwelling does not rise as rapidly as the price of land per acre. Town and country planning controls may frustrate this tendency for more houses to be built on very high-cost land, but, in recent years, we have seen how economic pressures have built up and forced a reconsideration of planning densities which were laid down in a period of rent controls, when the price of land was artificially deflated.

During the period 1945–55 the price of land relative to the cost of building was very much lower than it had been before the First World War. This was partly due to bombing, which increased the supply of building land, but in many of our large cities was due to the influence of rent control. Table 32 gives some examples of the ratio of the price of land to the total cost of development for houses built by the L.C.C. between 1895 and 1908.

Between 1895 and 1907 the L.C.C. built twenty housing estates and and on average the land cost 34·4 per cent of the total costs of development. Some of the sites which were bought were very expensive slum-clearance sites in places like Holborn, but many of the estates were built on much cheaper land in the East End or south of the Thames.

During the period 1919–39, the cost of land as a proportion of the total cost of L.C.C. housing projects fell to an average of about 25 per cent. Some estates were built on very much more costly land, but on average the price of land appears to have been significantly less (relative to the cost of building) than at the end of the nineteenth century. After 1945, many of the L.C.C. building programmes were carried out on land which was relatively cheap; often the land cost was 10 per cent or less of the total development costs and on average the cost of land may have fallen to less than 15 per cent of the total costs of development.

*Table 32: Land cost as a percentage of the total cost of development.*[1]

| Date of development | Estate | Land cost to total cost |
|---|---|---|
| | | % |
| 1895 | Goldsmith Row | 40·2 |
| 1895 | Deptford | 17·8 |
| 1900 | Shoreditch | 32·3 |
| 1900 | Limehouse | 19·0 |
| 1905 | Wemlake | 56·7 |

While the figures which have been examined strongly suggest that the price paid for land in the immediate post-war period was unusually low, it would be dangerous to draw too firm a conclusion from this limited evidence (because many of the sites were bombed and sold for a very low price). Without a survey which covered the whole of the country and took into consideration not only local-authority building but also private-enterprise building, it is only possible to come (very tentatively) to the conclusion that the present apparently high prices paid for land within and around London are in fact only bringing land values back to the relative position they occupied in the nineteenth century.

In considering the price of land in relation to the general level of income, and the situation of a particular piece of land, it will normally be found that the richest members of the population will bid up the price of the most desirable pieces of land, so that the price of the land plus the building on the land is approximately equal to three or four times the annual income of the man who bids for the land. Thus, if a few families have an income of £10,000 a year, while a majority of families have an income of £1,000 a year, those with the highest income are likely to bid anything up to £30,000 or £40,000 for a house which they wish to occupy. Those with an average income of £1,000 are likely to bid the price of houses up to £3,000 or £4,000. As, however, the

1. *Housing by Local Authorities*, British Parliamentary Papers 1915, vol. LIV, 1914–16.

number of very rich people in any society is proportionately very small, they affect only a small part of the total land market. The incomes of the very rich determine the price of land in places such as Westminster and Chelsea, but it is the average income which determines the price of land in areas like Orpington and the suburbs of Birmingham. The actions which cause land prices to rise do not stem from land speculators, who merely take advantage of rising prices and do not actually cause them. Variable and high land prices are the natural consequence of an uneven distribution of income and a very large demand for the limited number of dwellings available.

During the period 1951–61, the stock of dwellings in the Greater London area was renewed at the overall rate of 1·2 per cent per annum. Over the ten-year period therefore 12 per cent of the total stock of dwellings was newly built. About half of these were built by local authorities, which means that only 6 per cent of the 1961 stock of dwellings were new houses which were available to purchasers in the open market.

Under these conditions, it is hardly surprising that the richest 20 per cent of the population felt the existence of a shortage and the majority of the people suffered from a very acute shortage indeed. The shortage of new dwellings was met by the conversion and improvement of older dwellings, particularly in places like Chelsea, Westminster, St Marylebone and Kensington. The very high price for land which is paid in these boroughs is a reflection of the fact that for every house or flat there are many people trying to obtain the right to live in the property. As the demand cannot be satisfied in the traditionally popular places, it overflows into boroughs such as Hampstead, Paddington and Lambeth. As the rather richer people move to these areas the middle-income families move farther out and populate places on the outskirts of the metropolis.

The families with less than average income tend to be squeezed into the ring between the inner boroughs and the outer suburbs. The demands of this group are most often and most cheaply met by the use of the older houses built for the middle-income groups seventy or a hundred years before. If these houses can be subdivided they are particularly likely to be occupied by the poorer families, because three poor families can pay an aggregate rent for one house which is higher than the rent which one family in the middle-income group could afford to pay. Middle-income families have the choice of either being crowded into a small amount of space in the centre of a large town or moving to the suburbs. Many of them make the choice to move out to the suburban areas where they can afford to rent three or four times as much space as they would be able to rent in the centre. The poorer families do not have this choice as they cannot afford to live very far from their work, and they would have to live a very long way out of central London to find something cheap enough for them to buy or rent. Thus in the centre of large cities one can expect to find a more uneven distribution of income than in the outlying suburbs. The income statistics of the Inland Revenue for 1959–60 unfortunately relate to the areas in which income is 'earned' and not to the areas where the income holders live. They cannot therefore be used to examine the hypothesis that the rich and the poor have stayed in London while the middle-income group have moved out. Further research is urgently needed on this question, because an intelligent building programme and local-authority rents policy can only be formulated on the basis of income levels of each locality.

# CHAPTER 10

# A General Housing Subsidy

In the earlier chapters, the four ways in which government aid is given to occupiers of houses has been given. The four methods of aiding householders are quite separate and uncoordinated and owe more to the accidents of history than to present economic and social needs or possibilities. The present state-assistance to housing is:

1. Tax relief given to owner-occupiers on the interest paid on their mortgages.
2. Direct subsidies given to local authorities and some housing associations.
3. The indirect aid which is given to tenants by rent control.
4. Tax relief to housing associations and on the profits of local authorities.

The first of these forms of government help was introduced quite absent-mindedly about 150 years ago, when there were very few owner-occupiers. The second was introduced about seventy years ago, when local authorities were first empowered to subsidize their housing estates from the rate fund. Rent control was introduced fifty years ago, and the last forms of aid were introduced in 1963 and 1965.

The withdrawal of security of tenure from a number of families between 1957 and 1964 was socially disastrous because this removal was not accompanied by reforms of the other types of aid. The 1957 Rent Act was seen as a self-contained part of the national housing policy and as having no inter-related effects upon the other tenure groups. Many people who voted for the lifting of rent controls in 1957 did so in the belief that it would lead to an increase in the availability of houses to let. That this belief was quite unfounded has been shown in the Milner Holland Report[1] and in *English Housing Trends*,[2] and for those who knew of the tax position of private landlords the statistical evidence of a post-1957 fall in the number of dwellings to let came as no surprise.

1. Report of the Committee on Housing in Greater London, Cmnd 2605, H.M.S.O., 1965.
2. Cullingworth, op. cit.

As, however, the full impact of government policies is still not generally understood, a brief outline of post-war housing history is given below. For a more detailed account of the Acts the reader is referred to Appendix I of the Milner Holland Report.

1946  Increased subsidies to local authorities.
      Strict control over all building.
      Introduction of limited protection for tenants of furnished accommodation.
1949  'Improvement Grants' for houses with life of thirty years.
      Local authorities given unequivocable right to build for all income groups.
1952  Increased subsidies to local authorities.
1954  Protection granted to tenants of leasehold property.
      Increases in controlled rents.
      'Improvement Grants' made available to houses with life of fifteen years.
1955  Introduction of derequisitioning.
      Small decrease in subsidies to local authorities.
1956  Withdrawal of subsidy for general needs.
1957  Consolidation of housing law in new Act.
      Increase in rents of controlled property.
      Decontrol of some property.
1958  Temporary Act delaying impact of 1957 Rent Act until 1961.
1959  Building Societies given right to borrow £100 million from Exchequer at $\frac{1}{2}$ per cent below current interest. Loans to be made from this fund for purchase by future owner-occupiers of houses built *before* 1919.
      'Standard Grant' introduced for improvements to houses.
      Permission given to local authorities to lend up to 100 per cent of the valuation of a house.
1960  Extension of time granted to local authorities having difficulty in derequisitioning houses.
1961  Introduction of the 'resource test' for local-authority housing subsidies.
      Re-introduction of subsidy for general needs.
      Stricter rules introduced for the management of houses in multi-occupation.
      Fund of £25 million set up for housing associations.
1962  Further legislation on information to be written into rent books.
1963  Abolition of Schedule A.

Appointment of Milner Holland Committee to examine position of rented housing in London.

Reform of tax position of co-ownership housing associations.

1964 Introduction of 'control orders' for individual houses not being properly managed.

Local authorities given the right to enforce compulsory improvement of rented dwellings.

1965 Protection from eviction granted to tenants.

Recontrol of many tenancies and the introduction of a system of setting 'fair' rents.

Return, by way of grant, of taxes paid by housing associations which build houses to let.

Looking back on this calendar of housing events two things are very noticeable. First, the empirical process by which an attempt is made to achieve a particular goal. For instance, in 1949 new improvement grants were made available for houses with a life of thirty years. Landlords did not, however, make use of these grants and the length of expected life of the houses was shortened to fifteen years. A wholly irrelevant solution to the problem since, as is shown in Chapter 3, the reason why landlords did not make improvements was because after the payment of tax they could not make a sufficient return on their own part of the capital. The Government borrows the money for improvement grants over twenty years, and it is ironic that during the period over which the Government repays its loan, landlords pay back to the Government (in tax) almost the whole of the grant which they receive. In 1961 and 1964 the Government greatly strengthened the powers of local authorities to enforce improvements on landlords. We cannot, however, expect these improvements to be done until the taxation of rent revenue from residential property is brought into line with modern methods of financing such investments. We have in effect taxed bathrooms, modern kitchens and other improvements out of existence as far as privately rented property for the low-income groups is concerned. This is of even greater significance when it is remembered that for fifty years Governments in this country have controlled the revenue of such houses and through public-health and housing laws have attempted to control the expenditure; no Government has made any proper assessment of the relationship between expenditure and revenue, they have merely been content to tax at the fullest possible rate any surplus made regardless of its size.

Both Conservative and Labour Governments have, however, made departure from rented accommodation fairly easy to manage. A not untypical example of this is found in the period 1957 to 1960. The 1957 Rent Act freed some rents but the 1958 Act delayed the full impact of the earlier one and before the market had adjusted to the decontrol of rents a capital fund of £100 million was set aside to help ex-controlled rent tenants to buy the old rent-controlled property. As the £100 million was set aside for pre-1919 houses, the Government must have intended by this Act to reduce the stock of rented accommodation since the only pre-1919 houses against which the £100 million of capital could have flowed were those previously rented. By 1961 (when the 1957 Rent Act began to bite) a chaotic condition existed in the property markets of large cities like London and Birmingham. Demand for houses had been enhanced not only by the government provision of capital but also by a tremendous increase in new mortgages advanced by building societies, which grew from £370 million in 1958 to £548 million in 1961. Over the same period there had been an increased demand for dwellings by local authorities because of (a) derequisitioning from 1955 to 1961, (b) increased demolition of slums from 1954 to the present day and (c) actions taken to counter the impact of the decontrol of rents. As rent decontrol was intended to raise rents it is difficult to understand such action as the Westminster City Council's in buying the flats in Dolphin Square to prevent the tenants paying a free market rent. From the economic point of view, what such action achieved was the direction of still more capital on to an already over-burdened housing market.

On the supply side of the equation little had been done to increase the supply of dwellings. Local-authority subsidies had been reduced, and the reconsideration of land densities, which had been determined by aesthetic rather than economic criteria, was very slow. Late in the period (1961) housing associations were encouraged to increase the supply of houses, but it was not until 1963 and 1965 that their tax position was altered so that they could supply accommodation at cost. Thus their contribution has so far been very small. Private builders have been free to build when land and capital has been available, but their interest has for obvious reasons been in the building of houses for sale. Private landlords in central London boroughs have undertaken a very large amount of redevelopment, but the delay in operation of the 1957 Rent Act meant that many of them were unable to get possession of sites until 1961 to 1963, and the property which they are building is not likely to come on to the market until the period 1964 to 1966. Thus, from all sources of supply except the private building of houses for sale, the decade 1957 to 1967 can be seen as a period of re-thinking, adjustment to changing situations (legal, financial and fiscal), replanning, demolition and only ultimately of rebuilding.

The empirical approach to housing problems has resulted in a simultaneous attack upon the old supply of dwellings from two directions. The top end of the property market is being drastically renewed and modernized at exactly the same period as the local authorities are carrying out a major slum-clearance programme. Some boroughs of London in the period 1963 to 1965 were reminiscent either of the blitz or perhaps even of large prairie tracts one associates with the United States. Acres of land in boroughs such as Paddington and Camberwell have been cleared for comprehensive redevelopment, and this must clearly have led to a peak loss of supply as demolition got under way. There is necessarily a considerable time-lag between the moment when a house is vacated for demolition and the final demolition, rebuilding and reoccupation of the land. It may well be that an over-ambitious programme of demolition in London during the early sixties led to land being unoccupied for an average period of perhaps three to four yours. If to the two reasons directly connected with housing (rebuilding both for the wealthier groups in society and slum clearance) are added the large-scale road- and school-building programmes of the decade which have resulted in the demolition of many dwellings, the loss in the supply of accommodation must have reached major proportions and be one of the most important reasons for the severe housing difficulties found particularly in London.

The second thing to consider in looking at the housing legislation is the undesirable way in which something new is introduced every year. This must be regarded as a symptom of an intense nervous anxiety on the part both of the officials and the Government at the lack of success of each individual policy. Much of the post-war housing legislation is reminiscent of the proverbial squirrel in a cage going round and round in circles. This is partly because it is impossible to achieve 'better' housing more cheaply than inferior housing, and the electorate have not been willing to face this fact, but it has also been due to the continued hope on the part of the Conservative party that housing could be left to free market forces. On the other hand, the Labour party has taken a very casual view of the decline of the private landlord and would clearly be extremely reluctant to see any legislation introduced that aided the private landlord as opposed to curbing and controlling him. As, however, central-government aid to housing is now a permanent feature of government activity, it could with great benefit be given a more co-ordinated and less controversial position on the statute books. This is, however, unlikely to be achieved until a method is found and accepted by both political parties of achieving the following fundamental objectives:

1. A rational system of giving financial aid in such a manner that families with an average and above average income pay for their own accommodation without subsidy, while all families with a less than average income receive a carefully scaled subsidy given to meet their particular housing needs.
2. The introduction of one system of subsidies which is equitable as between different tenure groups. All families should be treated alike regardless of whether they are council tenants, owner-occupiers or the tenants of private landlords.
3. The introduction of a scheme which is equitable as between different types of owner. In particular the taxation of the revenue derived from dwellings should be the same whether the owner is an individual occupier, a local authority, a housing association or private company, or an individual landlord.
4. All taxes and subsidies should be related to the flow of capital to the housing market as a whole. An increase in capital funds unaccompanied by an increase in the supply of houses should be carefully avoided by a central body responsible for the overall co-ordination of a national housing programme.

*The role of the average income*

The average level of income plays an extremely important part in determining the average level of rent. In using the term 'average level of income' we mean here the average income for a husband with an average-size family. On average, builders will build houses for sale to, or rental by, families of average size with an average income. Families with more than the average income of their district will bid up the price of house-room so that they either obtain more than the average amount of space or live in the small areas which are regarded as highly desirable residential districts. However, in the United Kingdom only about 20 per cent of families are significantly richer than the majority of families and the distribution of income is, for housing purposes, remarkably 'equal'. This is partly because people regard housing as a long-term purchase; they buy or rent in accordance with the average income over their life-span, and not just with regard to a peak period of maximum earnings when they are in the prime of life and often have fewer family responsibilities. This means that while, quite obviously, rich families can bid up the price of land and houses, they do not thereby exclude the family with average income from obtaining a house.

In an absolutely free market, skilled and unskilled workers in regular employment would be able to obtain accommodation within their means, but the very poor (the retired, the sick, those in casual employment) would tend to be squeezed out of the market by those with an average income. For this reason, when thinking about a subsidy policy, care should be taken to direct the subsidy towards people in the lower-income brackets and to raise their income (for housing purposes) to the level of the average income of the district. This may have been the original purpose of all housing subsidies, but this objective has been much neglected in recent years.

Many of the tenants of local authorities are skilled workers and semi-skilled workers obtaining an income which is roughly equivalent to the national average income. If these tenants have their average income increased further by an average subsidy of £20 to £70 (see page 103) a year, it does not only mean that the taxpayers' money is being given to people who do not have a pressing need for it; it also means that the economic position of the poorest people is actually being worsened. When a local authority decides to buy land and accepts an estimate for the erection of houses, the local authority is contributing to the determination of the general level of land prices and the cost of building. If, therefore, a local authority decides that it can buy land and build houses which it will let at a net rent of £3 a week, plus a subsidy of say £2 a week, the local authority is itself contributing to the overall demand for land and buildings and pushing prices of accommodation up to the general level of £5 a week. If local authorities only subsidized families with less than the average income, the level of the average income would be the major determining factor in setting rents. The task of each local authority would be a very sensitive one of assessing the market and of avoiding any action which could push the price of houses and land above the level which the average family could afford to pay.

In towns where there is little shortage of land and no overall shortage of houses, this is what local authorities are already doing; but in all the big cities, where there is an acute shortage of building land and of dwellings, the local authorities have in recent years been forcing prices up against themselves and against the poorer residents.

When a local authority is prepared to buy a Victorian house with a life of twenty years for a price which necessitates an annual housing subsidy of £150, the local authority is pushing the price of all Victorian houses beyond the reach of the majority of families living in the neighbourhood.

The subsidy given to owner-occupiers through the tax system has exactly the same effect. This can be seen by reconsidering the data given in Chapter 5. If without tax concessions a house can be bought on mortgage for an annual outgoing of £287, this will fix the capital price of the house and land at about £3,500 to £3,900. If £287 was the maximum amount which most families could afford to pay, the price of most houses in a free market would be less than £4,000. When, however, some families can get their income-tax payments reduced by making mortgage repayments, those families will be able to bid up the price of the house and contract to pay, say, £350 in mortgage repayments, knowing that they will get back £50 to £60 through the tax concession.

Thus the tax relief raises the capital value of houses and makes it more difficult for the poorer families to obtain a house, because the richer families not only have higher incomes but also have incomes sufficiently high to entitle them to tax relief on interest payments. A housing policy should be designed in general to allow the richer families the full benefit of their higher incomes while making quite sure that they obtain no benefit at all by tax concessions.

In this way the range of rents would be kept down to the level which could be afforded without any subsidy by families with average incomes. These families should be the ones which set the levels of rent and, in so far as it is possible, the richer people should be persuaded to spend their income on cars, holidays, jewellery or clothes, etc., rather than upon land and property which it is socially necessary to distribute fairly evenly over the whole population. In areas of very acute housing shortage, it may be necessary to impose a special tax on houses in order to persuade people to use as little land as possible and to encourage them to make full use of existing houses and flats.

The general justification for taxing all residential property as opposed to subsidizing it is that a house yields a real income to the occupier, and so the owner-occupier of a house has a greater capacity to pay tax than the man who has the same money income but no house of his own. No one could deny that a house does yield a substantial real income to the owner who occupies it, and therefore on the general principle of taxing all income, a tax on owner-occupied houses can be justified.

However, the present housing situation is so bad in many of our big towns that it hardly seems a propitious moment for Chancellors to draw increased revenue from houses. If we are to take the national housing situation seriously and try in the next ten years to escape from the chronic shortage of modern accommodation, houses should perhaps not be taxed. When and if all houses have bathrooms and proper modern sanitation and heating, taxes can and no doubt will again be imposed on all houses. In the meantime, it would be unwise to do anything which would discourage the building and purchase of houses by families with average incomes. Another good reason against taxing dwelling-houses is the method by which local authorities in the United Kingdom raise revenue. As local rates are a direct tax upon dwellings, this already imposes a financial burden upon all households and it seems reasonable to leave dwellings as a source of tax revenue to local authorities.

*Subsidies*

It is very much harder to design a system of subsidies than a system of taxation. This is particularly so for housing as all subsidies of a commodity in fixed supply merely tend to raise the price of that commodity. If every family with less than the average national income were given a housing subsidy in cash, this would raise all rents and house prices and only landlords and sellers of land would benefit. Exactly the same situation would arise if a large group of people had their interest rate subsidized, obtained a grant covering the deposit for a house on mortgage or finally if the Government introduced some scheme by which a large number of people were entitled to obtain 100 per cent loans on the purchase price of their houses. Thus in introducing a general subsidy caution has to be exercised and generosity kept in check.

The obvious field in which a general housing subsidy could be most efficiently introduced would be the local-authority sector. This is because local authorities already allocate their houses to those in need and the introduction of a general subsidy would do nothing to alter the present method of allocation. A simple method of assisting these tenants would be by the removal of all subsidies from their landlords and the grant of subsidy directly to the tenants.

Each tenant could be given the statutory right to a housing allowance. The allowance to be related to the tenant's family responsibilities, level of rent and income. Each local authority would set its rents to cover all the current annual costs of the property held by the authority. The individual rent for any one property would bear no relation to the historic cost of that particular dwelling but would be set at the discretion of the local councillors so that it reflected the amenities of the dwelling. The only compulsion imposed upon local authorities would be that their aggregate rental income covered their aggregate annual outgoings, and that over a five-year period neither profit nor loss was made.

Tenants could then claim a housing allowance from some authority such as the Ministry of Pensions and National Insurance, which already deals with claims from people who have a statutory right to receive weekly payments such as pensions. The administrative organization of such a scheme should be very simple. The tenant could collect a claim form from his local post office which would be sent to the local office of the Ministry selected as the paying agent. When the tenant was entitled to receive a housing allowance the order book authorizing the post office to pay the allowance each week could be issued to cover a period of three or six months. The Ministry of Pensions and National Insurance are now considering alternative ways[1] of paying pensions, and if they decide to introduce a thirteen-week order-book for all pensioners, the system could easily incorporate the payment of housing allowances. Extra staff needed for this work could be recruited from the staff of housing departments, which at present administer rent rebate or differential rent schemes. If one Ministry with local offices was made responsible for the payment of all direct housing subsidies through allowances there should be a considerable saving of both staff and office accommodation. At present many local authorities keep files for rent rebate purposes on tenants who are also in receipt of pensions and National Assistance. Thus for one pensioner details may be kept in three offices and each office arranges for some aid to the pensioner. Not only would the new arrangement bring some economy into the administration of housing subsidies but it would also make it much easier for the poorer families to understand the system and obtain the aid to which they were entitled.

The level of housing allowances must depend upon fact and not magic. It is absurd for a rent rebate scheme to depend upon some number such as a fifth or a seventh of income as being a 'reasonable' level of income to spend upon rent. This is only an intelligible approach

1. See *The Times*, 28 July 1965.

if it is made by a commercial undertaking which wishes to make some assessment of the amount tenants are likely to be willing to pay for accommodation. The private landlord or building society is not directly concerned to help the poorest members of society, and when they reckon that a tenant or borrower can pay up to 20 or 25 per cent of their income towards housing costs, they are making this rough calculation on two fundamental assumptions: (1) that the individual concerned has an average or above average income, and (2) that he does not have a large number of dependants. Local authorities cannot operate upon these assumptions and they should not therefore operate upon a rule of thumb fraction of income to be spent on rent.

If the intention of a state housing subsidy is to allow the poorer than average to enjoy housing conditions similar to those with average incomes, the subsidy has to be varied in exactly the same way as the National Assistance Board scale rates are varied for families of different size. If the Ministry of Housing issued a scale of family basic expenditure each year, the level of housing allowances for any one family could be calculated as in Table 33.

*Table 33: 'Basic expenditure' required by families of various sizes (figures selected as an example of the way the scheme would operate).*

| Size of family | Basic expenditure £ s. d. | | |
|---|---|---|---|
| Single person | 5 | 0 | 0 |
| Husband and wife | 7 | 5 | 6 |
| Husband and wife, 1 child | 10 | 8 | 0 |
| Husband and wife, 2 children | 11 | 15 | 0 |
| Husband and wife, 3 children | 13 | 2 | 0 |
| Husband and wife, 4 children | 14 | 9 | 0 |
| Husband and wife, 5 children | 15 | 16 | 0 |
| Husband and wife, 6 children | 17 | 3 | 0 |

*Calculation of housing allowance*
*Example 1:* Husband and wife with three dependent children.

| | £ | s. | d. |
|---|---|---|---|
| Gross weekly income (excluding family allowance) | 15 | 7 | 6 |
| 'Basic expenditure' | 13 | 2 | 0 |
| Balance available for housing | 2 | 5 | 6 |
| Actual gross rent | 3 | 15 | 0 |

| | s. | d. |
|---|---|---|
| *Housing allowance* | 19 | 6 |

*Example 2:* Husband and wife with six dependent children.

|  | £ | s. | d. |
|---|---|---|---|
| Gross weekly income (excluding family allowance) | 15 | 7 | 6 |
| 'Basic expenditure' | 17 | 3 | 0 |
| Balance available for housing | | NIL | |
| Actual gross rent | 4 | 4 | 0 |
|  | £ | s. | d. |
| *Housing allowance* | 4 | 4 | 0 |

The table of basic family expenditure would cover items such as food, clothing, heating, travel, National Insurance contributions, papers, TV and other standard items purchased by 75 per cent of the population. It would need to be revised annually from the Ministry of Labour statistics of income and expenditure. Families obtaining retirement pensions and at present obtaining help through an N.A.B. grant would automatically be entitled to a housing allowance covering the full amount of their rent and rates.

The proposed housing-allowance scheme has the merit of simplicity, directness of impact and privacy. It would be churlish to label it a 'means test' system. The scheme is based upon 'expenditure needs' and not simply upon levels of income. It also gives to tenants the right to a housing allowance which they do not at present enjoy. The resentment felt by many tenants when a 'means test' is suggested does not rest only upon memories of the 'charity' of past generations but also upon the fairly harsh experience of present-day local-authority rent rebate schemes. The Greater London Council scheme for social aid is a fairly typical example of the undesirability of leaving an assessment of rent-paying capacity to extremely busy councillors. In the scheme introduced in 1965, the G.L.C. accepted a proportion of one seventh as the 'right' amount of income for families to spend on net rent, but such a figure could easily result in extreme hardship for many of the families which most require housing subsidies.

The present N.A.B. scale rates of assistance are usually accepted as giving the basic minimum required for food, clothing and heating, etc., by families of different sizes, and we would not expect any rent rebate scheme to leave a family with less than these basic rates. However, under the Greater London Council scheme, and many other similar local-authority schemes, families with four or more children may be charged a rent which leaves them with a balance for things

11

other than housing which is below the N.A.B. rate. For example, if a tenant was earning a gross income of £15 7s. 6d., under the G.L.C. scheme he would pay a net rent of £2 3s. 11d. plus general and water rates of approximately £1 regardless of the number of children which he had. From his gross income of £15 7s. 6d., 19s. 1d. is deducted for National Insurance and Graduated Pension, which leaves him with a 'take home' pay of £14 8s. 5d. If he has four children the family allowance is 28s. per week, which gives him a total cash income of £15 16s. 5d. per week. Deducting £3 3s. 11d. from this for rent and rates, he is left with £12 12s. 6d. to cover all non-housing expenditure. The 1965 N.A.B. scale rate for this family is £12 2s., so that if the tenant has to pay fares to work in excess of 2s. 2d. per day the family will be living below the N.A.B. rates.

As the N.A.B. rates are only intended to cover short periods of family difficulties and not a prolonged period, they make no allowance for the purchase and renewal of furniture or the provision of working clothes. Thus to live at the N.A.B. rates for several years must be to live in dire poverty and to live below it must be almost impossible. Many local authorities complain about their large 'problem' families which do not pay their rent regularly. A careful comparison of the rent rebate schemes and the N.A.B. rates will usually explain the arrears and suggest that the punishment of eviction for arrears of rent is scarcely justified.

In the housing allowance scheme which has been proposed in this chapter, recognition would be given to the fact that there are only a very small percentage of really large families and that many of the fathers of these families earn low incomes. During the infancy of their children a housing allowance which covered the whole of their rent would be a cheaper and more humane way of aiding the children than by either depriving them through high rents of council housing or taking the children into care. Many of the problems of juvenile delinquency are directly related to poverty and poor housing, and it is only through a housing allowance scheme of the type suggested that both the more extreme forms of poverty and poor housing can be eradicated at a relatively low cost. An overall increase in family allowances would not achieve the same objective, first because not all large families are in financial need and secondly because a flat-rate increase regardless of need merely tends to push up the price of houses and land.

The G.L.C. scheme has been discussed at some length because, when it was first introduced, it received much favourable publicity and no paper criticized it on the grounds that it left the large family in considerable economic difficulty. Many people assumed that if only a seventh of income is taken for rent it must be all right for all families of all sizes. Only the tenants and their wives see the fallacy of using numbers to assess a rent-paying capacity, and as large families only represent about one per cent of all council tenants their protests are easily neglected. Councils which do not have as generous a scheme as the G.L.C. and take a sixth of their tenants' income as basic rent, squeeze even the more average-sized family with a low income of £12 to £14 per week.

If the electorate fully understood the nature of the proposed housing allowance scheme and the fact that it started by allowing each family sufficient to cover non-housing expenditure, there is no reason why it should not be acceptable to both the majority of council tenants and the majority of electors. Once accepted by council tenants it could be easily extended to owner-occupiers if building societies agreed to co-operate by continuing their present policy of only granting loans to 'credit worthy' applicants. If the introduction of a housing allowance scheme induced the societies to be lax about the grant of loans, on the assumption that if the borrower did not pay the interest the Government would, the scheme would rapidly collapse as the total bill for housing allowances increased. There is, however, little doubt that the societies would co-operate with the Government and only lend to people in regular employment and with genuine prospects of repaying the whole of the loan. The extension of the scheme to owner-occupiers would relieve the owners of the anxieties of defaulting on their mortgages after an unexpected family misfortune, such as the illness of the head of the household, which makes it necessary for him to take an unskilled, poorly-paid job.

Finally, the tenants of private landlords could be brought into the scheme if rents were controlled at a level regarded as 'fair' by both the Government and the landlord. Under the Rent Act 1965 regulated and controlled rents are likely to be thought 'fair' by the Government, but it is doubtful whether landlords will regard them in quite such a favourable light.

The difficulty about the word 'fair' is that it stems from undefined views about equity. It has for instance been suggested above that it would be 'fair' for a tenant with three children and a gross income of £15 7s. 6d. per week to pay in 1965 a gross rent of £2 5s. 6d. per week and to receive a housing allowance of 19s. 6d. per week. But this is not based upon the assumption that £2 5s. 6d. per week is a 'fair' rent or even that £3 5s. is the 'fair' rent. The rent of £3 5s. is neither fair nor unfair, it is simply the rent which it was assumed that a local authority would need to charge if neither profit nor loss was made on their housing account. The concept of 'fairness' is to be found in the twin assumptions that a family with three children required in 1965 at least £13 2s. plus 18s. family allowance for food, clothing, heating, etc., and that they also require accommodation of some minimum standard. The amount of rent to be paid is a residual from the first assumption and the money cost of supplying 'standard' accommodation is determined by the second.

If we had a general housing-allowance scheme for every family, a rent of privately-let accommodation could be set on the same principle as that suggested for setting local-authority rents. It was suggested that these should be set to cover all costs of holding the property. For local authorities this means the costs of servicing capital, carrying out maintenance, management and insurance. For private landlords 'all costs' include these four items plus the cost of retaining the investment. A private landlord does not need to keep his capital in houses to let and he will therefore compare the profits of keeping capital in alternative assets. For instance, if a landlord has a house which he could sell for £10,000 and he obtains a net rent (after all expenses) of £100, he would be sensible to sell the house and invest his money in some other asset, if this alternative asset gave him a net income of 5 per cent (i.e. £500). Thus, if an outside body imposes a maximum rent upon a private landlord, some careful thought should be given to the capital value of the house and to the returns on alternative investments.

Many people would claim that this would not result in 'fair' rents because the capital value of a house reflects the shortage of houses. This is true, but shortage of houses in relation to what? Presumably in relation to the incomes and needs of some poor families: those who are poorer than average and cannot afford to compete against the richer families. If during 1965 the average gross weekly income of householders in the south-east of England was £24 per week, the people with £24 or more per week would bid up the price of accommodation to £6 or over per week in a free market. This is because, in 1965, an average household could live on a pre-tax income of £16 to £18 after the payment of housing costs of £6 to £8 per week. Thus the shortage of dwellings and high average earnings have resulted in rents or mortgage repayments of £200 to £300 plus general rates of £50 to £150 per annum for the richest 50 per cent of the population.

It is the high weekly average income of £24 and the cost of essentials like food and clothing that creates the rents of £6 to £8. Rent is a residual and from rents the capital value of houses is determined.

If the richer half of the population has bid rents to a level that makes the average capital value of a standard house (i.e. a house with all modern amenities) be £5,000 for one letting, then it must follow that the average capital price of a sub-standard letting occupied by households with less than average incomes must be less than £5,000. It will normally be £5,000 minus the amount required to make it a 'standard' letting which the richer people would like to occupy. Thus, if someone was asked to value a sub-standard house, he should first estimate the costs of bringing it up to standard, then estimate with reference to the open market the capital value of the house when improved and repaired. If £3,000 was required to modernize an old house which would be sold for £5,000 when modernized, then it should be possible to find a buyer willing to give £2,000 for the house in its dilapidated condition. In setting rents for the sub-standard accommodation the capital value of the house would be the £2,000 present-condition value and a 'fair' rental value would be about £200 for the whole house. In London, where many of the sub-standard houses are in multi-occupation, this would result in rents per letting of £50 to £100 per annum—rents which are hardly excessive in relation to the incomes of unskilled manual and clerical workers who live in these houses.

An alternative method of imposing rents upon private landlords would be to take the average income of the tenants to whom the landlord lets his accommodation and find out how much the tenants are, on average, willing to pay. If, for instance, the landlords of a district specialized in letting rooms to unskilled workers earning £16 per week and on average the tenants paid £3 per week gross rent, then the rent level of this district could be set at £3 per week, but landlords could be forced to give accommodation of a minimum standard for this rental. As on average these tenants would require two rooms plus a kitchen, the average rent of £3 could be for this size of accommodation. This relationship between income of tenants, size of accommodation and rent would be thrown up by the market. The regulation of rents would come into play when (1) landlords were charging the rent of £3 for only one or two rooms, (2) supplying inadequate plumbing facilities, (3) maintaining the house inadequately, or (4) letting the accommodation to people with a lower income or larger families, thus obviously changing the character of the neighbourhood from one in which the average family of average size and average unskilled worker's income lives to one in which larger than average size families live with lower than average incomes. In this exercise the Government would in effect be saying to the landlords that they had freely chosen to let their dwellings to families with incomes of £16 per week and that the maximum rental that could be taken from such an income would be £3. If this rent was more than a tenant with a large family could pay, the Government would make up the difference by means of a housing allowance.

These two methods of setting rents give approximately the same results. An unmodernized Victorian terraced house which could be sold as it stands for £2,000 could alternatively be let at a rent of £200 plus £30 per letting for repairs and management. If there were three lettings of two rooms plus a kitchen, this would be a net rent of £100 per letting and the addition of rates would bring the rent to about £2 10s. to £3 per week—the same level of rent assessed by starting with the average tenant's income and expenditure on food, etc.

No difficulty should be experienced in the valuation of houses which are overcrowded. If the house is valued on the assumption that the public health laws and private legal contracts are observed, little difficulty should be experienced in valuing a house. Present very high prices paid by some purchasers of houses are a direct reflection of criminal overcrowding and the non-observance of building-society and local-authority mortgage contracts, which forbid the house purchaser to let off a part of the premises. Recently (July 1965) £6,000 was asked for a house with ten rooms in Camden Town by a landlord who assured prospective buyers that each room was let for 10s. per day and 10s. per night to shift workers, thus giving an income of £1 per twenty-four hours per room or £63 per week for the nine rooms which were let. These exceptional cases can clearly not form the basis for a rational system of valuing houses and should be discounted when trying to formulate a rational system of setting rents.

In the Rent Act published in 1965, the proposed method of setting 'fair' rents is by reference to a set of rules which define certain rents as 'fair' and set disputed rents by reference to those stated by definition to be 'fair'. The defined 'fair' rents are the rents of dwelling-houses situated in a locality where the number of persons seeking to become tenants is not 'substantially greater' than the number of dwellings available. One possible interpretation of this rule is that the rents of a small locality (say a block of fifty flats) could be defined as 'fair' if 10 to 20 per cent of these flats were empty and, at the rents set by the landlord, the flats were gradually let. But as new tenants came into the empty flats, other tenants left so that there was a continuous vacancy-rate of 10 to 15 per cent. It would then be clear that the number of persons seeking these flats was not substantially greater than the number of flats available. The rents of such flats could be said to be 'fair' by definition and could be standardized so as to become a 'reference' rent by means of which the rents of all other premises could be set.

The 'reference' rents would certainly be the rents of the most expensive flats because where rent regulation is needed it is only at the top end of the market that supply and demand at the current rent is such that a small vacancy-rate appears. If the vacancy-rate is large (say over 20 per cent) landlords might be induced to lower their rents, and similarly, if it was very low (say less than 5 per cent), landlords may wish to raise their rents. Thus, to find a market in equilibrium we have to select some vacancy-rate which shows simultaneously that (a) the number of persons seeking the flats is not substantially greater than the number of dwellings, and that (b) the landlord has no incentive to raise or lower his rents. To ensure both these conditions, a vacancy-rate lying between 10 and 15 per cent could be taken as a 'rule of thumb' method of ensuring equilibrium in the market.

Suppose we find such a market in central London, for instance some large block of flats in Westminster let at exclusive rents of £1,000 per annum. These rents would be defined as 'fair' because the market was in equilibrium (i.e. rents were neither rising nor falling and both landlords and tenants were content with the prevailing level). This rent can be standardized by listing the amenities of the flat and giving the rent as X$s$. per square foot of internal dwelling-space, including all passages, cupboards, bathrooms, etc. In 1964 in central London the flats described had a net rent per square foot of approximately 11$s$. The amenities of the flats included (1) self-contained dwelling; (2) bathroom; (3) w.c.; (4) kitchen; (5) cold-water supply; (6) hot-water supply; (7) central-heating facilities; (8) electric power points in each room; (9) lifts; (10) furnished landings and passages; (11) balcony; (12) garage; (13) garden; (14) external amenities (beautiful view); (15) nearness to shops and/or work, and/or places of entertainment. All these things the tenant obtained for 11$s$. per square foot of space occupied. From this it is argued that tenants with less amenities should pay a 'regulated' rent proportionately smaller than this 'fair' rent set by a market which has attained equilibrium.

At the bottom end of the property market we have some controlled rents which are approximately equal to 2*s.* per square foot of space. These rents are not likely to be defined as too high and may reasonably be taken as the lowest possible rents. Thus, by this system, those who set 'regulated' rents have a scale of rent levels which lies between 132*d.* and 24*d.* per square foot. The scale therefore has 108 units and the art of setting a rent will be the art of selecting a graduated table of amenity values. The table on the page opposite (Table 34) is given as an example of the type of matrix which might be used.

*Dwelling A:* New conversion in Victorian terraced house near to Holland Park in Kensington.

> External amenities: Very good district and good views from windows.
>
> Internal amenities: Kitchen with some fitted cupboards —new sink and draining board—old type of flooring which needs to be covered with lino.
> Hot water available from geysers— no central supply.
> No individual garage but covered parking space available and reserved for tenant of flat.

*Dwelling B:* Nineteenth-century mansion flat.

> External amenities: Not very good district of north London, but good transport facilities.
>
> Internal amenities: Kitchen as for dwelling A. Garden available for residents—well maintained by landlord.

*Dwelling C:* Nineteenth-century terraced cottage-type house.

> External amenities: Poor district near to a British Railway goods yard.
>
> Internal amenities: Kitchen has modern sink but no draining board—a cupboard for china, and ventilated food cupboard. No power points for cooker, refrigerator or iron. w.c. in back garden near to back door of house. Structure of w.c.—good. Small garden with properly maintained garden wall and facilities for hanging out washing.

*Table 34: Matrix table for setting net rents per square foot of space occupied in the London region.*

Eleven shillings per square foot of internal space is assumed, by definition, to be a 'fair' rent[1] of the dwelling described in the first line. The tenant is responsible for internal repairs and the payment of general and water rates. The Landlord is responsible for external repairs, the maintenance of halls, staircases, lifts, and the provision and maintenance of central-heating plant.

| Description of dwelling | External amenities | | INTERNAL AMENITIES | | | | | | | | | | | | | | TOTAL NET ANNUAL RENT |
|---|---|---|---|---|---|---|---|---|---|---|---|---|---|---|---|---|---|
| | London location | District location | Self-contained | Kitchen | Cold water | Hot water | Bath-room | W.C. | Electric points | Central heating | Balcony | Fitted wardrobes | Garage | Garden | Lift | Furnished landings | Per sq. ft. (given in pence) |
| 'Fair' Rent | 24 | 24 | 12 | 12 | 4 | 7 | 7 | 4 | 2 | 10 | 5 | 2 | 7 | 5 | 6 | 1 | 132 |
| A | 24 | 22 | 12 | 9 | 4 | 2 | 7 | 4 | 2 | 0 | 0 | 2 | 3 | 0 | 0 | 1 | 92 |
| B | 24 | 6 | 12 | 9 | 4 | 7 | 7 | 4 | 2 | 0 | 0 | 0 | 0 | 4 | 6 | 1 | 86 |
| C | 24 | 0 | 12 | 6 | 4 | 0 | 0 | 2 | 0 | 0 | 0 | 0 | 0 | 3 | 0 | 0 | 51 |
| D | 24 | 0 | 0 | 0 | 2 | 0 | 0 | 1 | 0 | 0 | 0 | 0 | 0 | 0 | 0 | 0 | 27 |

1. By December 1965 there was some evidence to suggest that these rents had risen to 15s.,–20s. per square foot.

*Dwelling D:* Nineteenth-century terraced house in multi-occupation. Each tenant has two rooms—four tenants in house.

> External amenities: Poor district—house backing on a factory making packing-cases.
>
> Internal amenities: Sink with cold-water tap on landing outside tenant's room.
>
> w.c. on landing below tenants' rooms—shared by all tenants of house.

The problems of composing a matrix of this type can be classified into two groups. First, the problem of minimum rent. In order to have some minimum rent there must always be one element in the matrix which is above zero. In the suggested matrix the only factor always above zero is the first external amenity (London location). If the rent for this amenity is fixed at 24*d.* it will yield a minimum rent of 2*s.* per annum per square foot of space. This gives a minimum rent of £28 per annum for two rooms with a gross floor area of 280 square feet (one room 10 x 10 feet and one room 15 x 12 feet). This is a typical letting in a London multi-occupied Victorian house and is clearly a rent well within tenants' rent-paying capacity. The existence of a shared bathroom or a sink in one room with proper provision for hot and cold water would push the rent up to about £49 per annum. (Fourpence for shared bath; 1*d.* for shared w.c.; 7*d.* for sink and draining-board in one room; 6*d.* for proper provision for hot and cold water supply. Total net rent: 1*s.* 6*d.* plus 2*s.* for location, which is 3*s.* 6*d.* per square foot per annum.) The illustrative matrix is assumed to relate to London and the first element of 24*d.* is the suggested minimum rent for space in London. The matrix for some other city or rural area would have some other smaller amount in the first constant column of the matrix. The determination of the amount to be entered into the first column does of course depend upon the definition of a 'fair' rent, but if this element is derived from the level of controlled rents in the town to which the matrix relates, both tenants and landlords might be willing to accept it as a minimum rent for the location factor.

The second problem which is apparent from the matrix is the distribution of pence per square foot for the different amenities. Each amenity has to be separately listed, and the rent to be fixed for a given amenity should bear some relation to the cost of providing the amenity. Thus, before drawing up a table of this type, a committee of experts on building and maintenance costs should cost each separate item and distribute the 132*d*. according to the proportionate cost of providing each separate internal amenity. The author has made no attempt to do this, and the matrix which is given is purely to illustrate the method of setting rents by reference back to rents discovered in that part of the property market which is in equilibrium.

The reader will notice that a high rating has been given to the quality of being self-contained, to kitchens and to central heating. Self-containment has been given a high rating because London flats are of varying degrees of separateness and it is important that the people who set rents should have quite a large scale upon which to manoeuvre.

A house may be, for instance, divided into two 'self-contained' lettings, but the top-floor tenant has the right to go through a ground-floor passage in order to get to his part of the garden. Thus, the top-floor tenant may enjoy a greater degree of self-containment than the ground-floor tenant. Alternatively, flats may have been made 'self-contained' with respect to sight but by no means with respect to sound because the partitions set up are very thin.

Kitchens and central heating have been given a high rating as it is assumed that, in flats with a rent of £1,000 per annum, the kitchens have every modern convenience, such as waste-masters, many well-designed cupboards, a suitable hard flooring and a large number of points for gas and electrical equipment. Central heating is assumed to cover the whole flat and to be of a modern and reliable type. All other amenities are assumed to be of a standard type.

Obviously the distribution suggested can be disputed; the question is not whether the given distribution is right but whether six experts in building costs could sit in committee and arrive at an agreed distribution which could, for the purpose of setting rents, be defined as 'reasonable'. Once these three exercises are completed—(1) Identifying the rent in the market which is in equilibrium, (2) setting the minimum rent to cover the location factor and (3) distributing the remainder among the other amenities—the problem of setting a rent for a particular dwelling is relatively simple. The question of whether or not a tenant has a kitchen is easily ascertained, and, by separating out the use of hot and cold water from the use of a kitchen, rents may fairly easily be set for tenement property where the tenant has only two rooms in one of which a sink has been installed. In any one particular case an ordinary group of men should be able to reach agreement about the total rent to be charged by reaching agreement upon each of the separate items.

Finally, we come to the two most difficult questions of all. First, do the rents set by this system discount the element of 'shortage'? Clearly they could be made to by ignoring the first two columns, which give a maximum rent in the illustrative matrix of 4s. for the locational factor. It would perhaps be possible to ignore the second column, which allows a maximum rent of 2s. per square foot for a view over St James's Park or some other particularly pleasing vista, but it would scarcely be possible to discount the first column, which is the one which gives the basic rent for any space in London.

The second question, which is almost unanswerable, is, will rents set by this method give landlords a sufficient revenue to induce them to retain and improve their property? There seems to be no reason why it should do so, although in the example given the minimum of 2s. per square foot has been selected partly with a view to ensuring that even in the worst property there shall be sufficient rent income to cover the costs of regularly cleaning the common parts of the house and maintaining the structure in a wind- and weatherproof condition. In the example given of rooms in a tenement let at a rent of £49 per annum, the total income from the dwelling-house would be £196 if there were four similar lettings in the house. If the landlord spent £80 per year on maintenance, management, cleaning and insurance he would have a taxable income of £116. After tax he would have a little over £68 if income tax was 8s. 3d. in the pound. At today's prices this is not a very large income and will be unlikely to persuade other landlords who have not installed a bathroom or sinks for each of their tenants to do so.

As private landlords are now the only type of house owner subject to the full weight of income, corporation and capital-gains tax, it might perhaps be possible to combine this method of setting regulated rents with some provision for the depreciation of residential property subject to a regulated rent. Alternatively, a special arrangement could be introduced so that different rates of tax were applied to income derived from heriditaments with a 'regulated' rental income (net of the expenses of repairs and management) of less than £50 and between £51 and £100, leaving the full rate of tax to be paid on rental income which exceeded £101. An arrangement of this type might persuade a few of the remaining landlords to retain cottage-type property and manage it properly until it was ready for demolition. The only alternative is an acceptance of the sale to owner-occupiers of small dwellings which will present many difficult problems of town redevelopment in five to fifteen years' time.

If this or the other suggested methods of setting 'fair' rents is introduced over the country, the suggested housing allowance scheme could be extended to the tenants of private landlords. In order to prevent tenants from renting dwellings which were well above their means, the housing allowance could be restricted to tenants with an annual income which did not exceed the national average earned income of husbands and their wives. At present this is approximately £22 per week, and by excluding those with a higher income it would prevent single people and married couples from renting accommodation at very high rents. Families with children are unlikely to be given the opportunity to occupy the higher regulated rent property as it would not be in the interests of landlords to let their property to large families, who are much more destructive than households which consist wholly of adults.

Some difficulties might occur if single, elderly people, living on a pension, rented property at regulated rents in the range £300 to £400 and claimed a housing allowance to cover a large proportion of the rent. To cope with this difficulty the officer with local responsibility for paying out housing allowances might be given the right to request the local authority of the district to find alternative cheaper accommodation for the tenant. Even if this was impossible in the short run, the fact that one organization was responsible for giving financial help to elderly people would mean that, in the long run, more effective provision for the elderly would be made, as giving financial aid specifically for housing would make the national government more directly concerned to economize on the most expensive space and persuade people to move to smaller accommodation when they no longer required two or three bedrooms.

*Conclusions*

The proposals which have been outlined in this chapter may appear to be a somewhat radical solution of the current problems of housing finance. They are however only a rationalization of the systems which are already used to subsidize housing. If the proposed reforms were accepted, Parliament would no doubt give the Ministry of Housing the duty of laying down the levels of housing allowances and the Ministry of Pensions (or other selected agent) would act only as the Ministry's agent in distributing them. Thus the system need not impose upon the paying-out agent any duties which are properly the responsibility of experts in the housing field.

The control of private rents and the grant of security of tenure are not new proposals and the suggestions made are merely that a sensible method of setting rents be introduced. It will be difficult, if not impossible, to do this rationally until a body of statistical knowledge is accumulated so that the officers of tribunals know the true annual costs of keeping houses available for letting. There is, however, no inherent difficulty in setting up a small research team to carry out continuous analysis and classification of housing costs and the decisions of tribunals. The results of such research could well be published monthly by the Ministry of Housing in the form of a 'Bulletin on Housing'.

The total costs of the proposed subsidy should be fairly small. The subsidies to owner-occupiers through housing allowances are unlikely to be large, at least in the early years of the scheme. If the tax relief allowed to the richer owner-occupiers was slightly reduced, the increased tax revenue derived from the reduction would probably cover the increased expenditure on direct subsidies to the poorer owners. (See Table 13, page 68, in Chapter 5 for the estimated proportion of individuals with incomes of less than £800 who were borrowers. While these figures are not very accurate, they give some estimate of the relatively small amount of borrowing for housing by the lowest income groups.)

The proposed method of subsidizing local-authority tenants is unlikely to result in a higher total subsidy to this group. It is possible that the Exchequer subsidy might rise, but this would be offset by a fall in rate subsidy. Any change in the total level of subsidy would depend upon the assessment of the minimum family income required before the payment of rent. If it is set at a high level then clearly the subsidy will be high. If, however, it is assumed that there are now some council tenants who earn more than the national average income and obtain a subsidy which they do not need, the proposal would result in a redistribution of subsidies.

The proposals involve giving all council tenants the *right* to a subsidy if they have an income which falls below a certain level. The state could hardly grant such a right unless it was accompanied by the state's *right* to withdraw the subsidy when income rose above the selected level. The fundamental difference between this scheme and the present local authorities' schemes of differential rents is that the proposal gives a genuine *quid pro quo*. Council tenants as individuals would be given the right to a subsidy. At present local authorities have the right to demand a higher rent when their tenants' incomes rise, but the tenants have no right with which they may demand a subsidy when their incomes fall. Thus the proposal which is put forward should be viewed rather as a suggestion for enhancing the status of tenants and giving them the same status already enjoyed by owner-occupiers. Whether or not the scheme will reduce the housing-subsidy bill is quite incidental. It is, however, only honest to admit that the present conjunction of economic circumstances is such that the proposals may, at least over a brief period, reduce the housing subsidies paid to council tenants.

The grant to other tenants of a right to a housing allowance would certainly increase the level of housing subsidies. Merrett and Sykes[1] have estimated that the cost would be £142 million per annum. This seems an unnecessarily high amount and is based upon the assumptions that (1) rent controls are removed and that (2) private tenants obtain the same average subsidy as present owner-occupiers. For reasons already given the author does not agree with the first policy recommendation and can see no reason why the second assumption should have been made. Housing subsidies are hardly a suitable vehicle for a state payment to everyone regardless of their need. If this was the purpose of housing subsidies, the simplest method would be to lower all tax payments and give no subsidies. If, however, the subsidies are to redistribute incomes from those with higher than average incomes to those with less, the subsidies have to be related directly to the needs of those with lower than average incomes. While it is now true that the average income *per family* living in council houses is higher than that per family in private lettings, the income *per person* is significantly higher for families in private lettings than in council dwellings. Thus it is not reasonable to assume from crude family-income statistics that tenants of private landlords necessarily need as much subsidy as council tenants. It is equally unreasonable to assume that they need as much as owner-occupiers; they may require less or more.[2]

It would not of course be wise to minimize the administrative problems which might arise in introducing a comprehensive scheme of this nature. The administrative difficulties are however a challenge, although a small one compared with the far greater difficulties of introducing income tax at the beginning of the nineteenth century and comprehensive national insurance, education and health schemes

1. A. J. Merrett and Allen Sykes, *Housing Finance and Development*, Longmans, Green, 1965.
2. For an estimate of the annual cost of such a scheme for 1966, see author's article, 'Meeting the Cost of Housing', *New Society*, 24 March 1966.

during the twentieth. The basis for a comprehensive housing scheme is already laid; all that is now needed is the will to bring the present possibilities to fruition. In future each individual should be able to choose the best type of house for his family knowing that his choice of tenure group would not influence the amount of state aid he obtained or the taxes he would have to pay. Each tenant or owner-occupier should be able to feel that the state will assist him with his housing costs during sickness, old age, unemployment and when his children are still at school if he has a low income, but that at all other times he will pay for his own housing. The state, in its turn, has a responsibility not to tax houses more heavily than other essential goods, and not to tax one source of income more heavily than others simply because it is derived from privately rented accommodation.

# Statistical Appendix One

Data from the 1959–60 survey of income carried out by the Inland Revenue. For information about the survey, see 105th Report of the Commissioners of H.M. Inland Revenue (Cmnd 1906), pages 81–201, and *Economic Trends*, No. 118, August 1963.

TABLE A

Survey of personal incomes (before tax) for 1959–60. Number of cases and deduction claimed for payment of interest to building societies *and* banks.

| Lower limit of income range | Number of cases | Aggregate interest deducted from income in thousands of pounds |
|---|---|---|
| £ | | |
| 50 | 6,673 | 380 |
| 100 | 12,417 | 698 |
| 150 | 9,346 | 494 |
| 180 | 6,816 | 390 |
| 200 | 22,077 | 1,261 |
| 250 | 30,202 | 1,502 |
| 300 | 39,140 | 1,755 |
| 350 | 52,875 | 2,692 |
| 400 | 66,497 | 3,286 |
| 450 | 88,285 | 4,231 |
| 500 | 122,581 | 5,814 |
| 550 | 157,328 | 7,595 |
| 600 | 187,173 | 8,784 |
| 650 | 208,484 | 10,249 |
| 700 | 208,600 | 10,577 |
| 750 | 203,344 | 10,519 |
| 800 | 186,356 | 9,889 |
| 850 | 171,053 | 9,321 |
| 900 | 157,374 | 8,931 |
| 950 | 143,817 | 8,182 |
| 1,000 | 476,642 | 29,386 |
| 1,250 | 209,679 | 14,923 |
| 1,500 | 97,883 | 7,647 |
| 1,750 | 57,753 | 4,990 |
| 2,000 | 64,308 | 5,819 |
| 2,500 | 34,811 | 3,503 |
| 3,000 | 36,683 | 4,162 |
| 4,000 | 17,195 | 2,291 |
| 5,000 | 8,691 | 1,265 |
| 6,000 | 8,224 | 1,447 |
| 8,000 | 3,853 | 892 |
| 10,000 and over | 5,736 | 2,843 |
| Gross nil | 706 | 140 |
| Neg: | 6,761 | 934 |
| Net nil | 6,288 | 396 |
| *Total, all ranges* | 3,115,651 | 187,188 |

TABLE B

Survey of personal incomes (before tax) for 1959–60. Number of cases and deduction claimed for payment of interest to insurance companies *and* ground rents *and* alimony, etc.

| Lower limit of income range | Number of cases | Aggregate deduction from income in thousands of pounds |
|---|---|---|
| £ | | |
| 50 | 9,545 | 293 |
| 100 | 20,164 | 443 |
| 150 | 16,987 | 374 |
| 180 | 11,342 | 162 |
| 200 | 36,438 | 716 |
| 250 | 44,932 | 808 |
| 300 | 47,103 | 792 |
| 350 | 46,502 | 891 |
| 400 | 53,928 | 1,038 |
| 450 | 66,745 | 1,266 |
| 500 | 77,667 | 1,558 |
| 550 | 95,137 | 1,963 |
| 600 | 104,612 | 1,944 |
| 650 | 112,733 | 2,082 |
| 700 | 110,445 | 2,183 |
| 750 | 106,619 | 2,198 |
| 800 | 100,560 | 2,281 |
| 850 | 89,938 | 2,087 |
| 900 | 82,463 | 2,032 |
| 950 | 77,180 | 2,017 |
| 1,000 | 253,675 | 8,039 |
| 1,250 | 127,737 | 5,914 |
| 1,500 | 72,775 | 4,306 |
| 1,750 | 49,437 | 3,717 |
| 2,000 | 62,425 | 5,743 |
| 2,500 | 38,635 | 4,616 |
| 3,000 | 45,011 | 7,070 |
| 4,000 | 22,880 | 5,297 |
| 5,000 | 12,940 | 3,770 |
| 6,000 | 13,550 | 4,664 |
| 8,000 | 6,601 | 3,447 |
| 10,000 and over | 10,758 | 12,767 |
| Gross nil | 3,245 | 975 |
| Neg: | 2,659 | 411 |
| Net nil | 7,372 | 244 |
| *Total, all ranges* | 2,040,740 | 98,108 |

TABLE C

Survey of personal incomes (before tax) for 1959–60. Number of cases and deduction claimed for property maintenance relief.

| Lower limit of income range | Number of cases | Aggregate deduction from income in thousands of pounds |
|---|---|---|
| £ | | |
| 50 | 624 | 23 |
| 100 | 1,159 | 34 |
| 150 | 1,610 | 41 |
| 180 | 1,086 | 30 |
| 200 | 5,487 | 209 |
| 250 | 10,094 | 258 |
| 300 | 12,655 | 271 |
| 350 | 13,793 | 265 |
| 400 | 14,345 | 276 |
| 450 | 16,926 | 313 |
| 500 | 16,478 | 337 |
| 550 | 19,019 | 365 |
| 600 | 21,940 | 461 |
| 650 | 21,414 | 423 |
| 700 | 23,221 | 491 |
| 750 | 22,422 | 409 |
| 800 | 20,495 | 447 |
| 850 | 19,875 | 424 |
| 900 | 18,435 | 462 |
| 950 | 18,272 | 402 |
| 1,000 | 72,197 | 1,678 |
| 1,250 | 49,424 | 1,368 |
| 1,500 | 33,371 | 1,017 |
| 1,750 | 24,977 | 933 |
| 2,000 | 35,313 | 1,428 |
| 2,500 | 24,320 | 1,132 |
| 3,000 | 30,228 | 1,924 |
| 4,000 | 16,105 | 1,093 |
| 5,000 | 9,221 | 1,479 |
| 6,000 | 9,439 | 1,477 |
| 8,000 | 4,808 | 894 |
| 10,000 and over | 7,792 | 3,857 |
| Gross nil | 80 | 11 |
| Neg: | 222 | 68 |
| Net nil | 395 | 7 |
| Total, all ranges | 597,342 | 24,307 |

**TABLE D**

Survey of personal incomes (before tax) for 1959–60. Number of cases of *married couples* making payment of interest to building societies *and* banks and claiming a deduction from their income in respect of such payments.

| Lower limit of income range £ | All married couples | Wife not earning | Wife earning | Percentage of wives earning |
|---|---|---|---|---|
| 50 | 2,234 | 1,542 | 692 | 31 |
| 100 | 4,707 | 3,270 | 1,437 | 31 |
| 150 | 2,807 | 1,984 | 823 | 29 |
| 180 | 1,143 | 703 | 440 | 38 |
| 200 | 3,978 | 1,239 | 2,739 | 69 |
| 250 | 7,582 | 1,714 | 2,868 | 38 |
| 300 | 12,460 | 7,267 | 5,193 | 42 |
| 350 | 21,857 | 13,575 | 8,282 | 38 |
| 400 | 35,027 | 22,700 | 12,327 | 35 |
| 450 | 57,733 | 41,551 | 16,182 | 28 |
| 500 | 93,341 | 67,517 | 25,824 | 28 |
| 550 | 129,827 | 92,577 | 37,250 | 29 |
| 600 | 162,595 | 120,247 | 42,348 | 26 |
| 650 | 187,629 | 133,847 | 53,782 | 29 |
| 700 | 189,909 | 133,612 | 56,297 | 30 |
| 750 | 187,683 | 128,296 | 59,387 | 32 |
| 800 | 174,178 | 113,207 | 60,971 | 35 |
| 850 | 160,641 | 96,698 | 63,943 | 40 |
| 900 | 148,019 | 83,832 | 64,187 | 43 |
| 950 | 136,859 | 70,301 | 66,558 | 49 |
| 1,000 | 456,063 | 218,207 | 237,856 | 52 |
| 1,250 | 199,510 | 97,516 | 101,994 | 51 |
| 1,500 | 92,656 | 50,588 | 42,068 | 45 |
| 1,750 | 54,346 | 33,059 | 21,287 | 39 |
| 2,000 | 59,837 | 35,949 | 23,888 | 40 |
| 2,500 | 32,062 | 19,250 | 12,812 | 40 |
| 3,000 | 33,581 | 20,328 | 13,253 | 39 |
| 4,000 | 15,594 | 9,711 | 5,883 | 38 |
| 5,000 | 7,817 | 5,188 | 2,629 | 34 |
| 6,000 | 7,282 | 5,139 | 2,143 | 29 |
| 8,000 | 3,418 | 2,576 | 842 | 25 |
| 10,000 | 5,011 | 3,948 | 1,063 | 21 |
| Gross nil | 495 | 369 | 126 | |
| Neg: | 3,175 | 2,724 | 451 | |
| Net nil | 2,476 | 1,982 | 494 | |
| *Total, all ranges* | 2,693,532 | 1,645,213 | 1,048,319 | 39 |

# Statistical Appendix Two

Total Subsidy (Exchequer and Rate) paid in 82 County Boroughs of England and Wales. The subsidy has been measured against the total amount of interest and capital repayment made on the Housing Account of each authority for the year 1962–63. The subsidy is given per £1 of interest and capital repayment made by the authority. Thus if one authority paid £90,000 in interest and £10,000 as repayment of capital in one year, and received an Exchequer subsidy of £20,000 and gave a subsidy from the General Rate Fund of £5,000, the total subsidy would be £25,000 measured against £100,000. This amounts to a 5s. subsidy for each £1 of debt charges.

TABLE A

*County Boroughs of England and Wales*

*All subsidies given per £1 of debt charges*

| Authority | Total subsidy | | Exchequer | | Rate | |
|---|---|---|---|---|---|---|
| | *s.* | *d.* | *s.* | *d.* | *s.* | *d.* |
| Merthyr Tydfil | 13 | 2 | 6 | 11 | 6 | 3 |
| Salford | 12 | 1 | 7 | 3 | 4 | 10 |
| Gateshead | 11 | 9 | 6 | 3 | 5 | 6 |
| West Ham | 11 | 4 | 5 | 5 | 5 | 11 |
| Blackburn | 10 | 10 | 5 | 0 | 5 | 10 |
| Bootle | 10 | 5 | 4 | 0 | 6 | 5 |
| Barrow-in-Furness | 10 | 2 | 4 | 1 | 6 | 1 |
| Birkenhead | 9 | 4 | 5 | 7 | 3 | 9 |
| Birmingham | 9 | 1 | 5 | 4 | 3 | 9 |
| Wakefield | 8 | 11 | 6 | 4 | 2 | 7 |
| Oldham | 8 | 11 | 5 | 4 | 3 | 7 |
| Kingston-upon-Hull | 8 | 8 | 5 | 7 | 3 | 1 |
| Grimsby | 8 | 7 | 5 | 3 | 3 | 4 |
| Burnley | 8 | 6 | 5 | 7 | 2 | 11 |
| Manchester | 8 | 5 | 6 | 1 | 2 | 4 |
| Stoke-on-Trent | 8 | 4 | 6 | 1 | 2 | 3 |
| Sheffield | 8 | 2 | 5 | 11 | 2 | 3 |
| Stockport | 8 | 1 | 5 | 6 | 2 | 7 |
| South Shields | 8 | 1 | 5 | 11 | 2 | 2 |
| Smethwick | 8 | 1 | 6 | 2 | 1 | 11 |
| Newcastle-upon-Tyne | 8 | 1 | 6 | 2 | 1 | 11 |
| Hastings | 8 | 1 | 5 | 7 | 2 | 6 |
| West Bromwich | 8 | 0 | 6 | 4 | 1 | 8 |
| Preston | 8 | 0 | 6 | 1 | 1 | 11 |
| Rochdale | 7 | 11 | 5 | 11 | 2 | 0 |
| Great Yarmouth | 7 | 9 | 6 | 6 | 1 | 3 |
| East Ham | 7 | 9 | 6 | 1 | 1 | 8 |
| Coventry | 7 | 9 | 5 | 9 | 2 | 0 |
| Sunderland | 7 | 8 | 5 | 8 | 2 | 0 |
| Halifax | 7 | 8 | 5 | 8 | 2 | 1 |
| York | 7 | 7 | 5 | 10 | 1 | 9 |
| Doncaster | 7 | 7 | 4 | 10 | 2 | 4 |
| Carlisle | 7 | 6 | 5 | 9 | 1 | 9 |
| Bradford | 7 | 6 | 5 | 8 | 1 | 10 |
| Dewsbury | 7 | 5 | 5 | 4 | 2 | 1 |
| Bolton | 7 | 5 | 5 | 9 | 1 | 8 |
| Rotherham | 7 | 4 | 5 | 4 | 2 | 0 |
| Leeds | 7 | 4 | 6 | 4 | 1 | 0 |
| Norwich | 7 | 1 | 6 | 1 | 1 | 0 |
| Wigan | 6 | 10 | 5 | 3 | 1 | 7 |

*Table A contd.*

| Authority | Total subsidy | | Exchequer | | Rate | |
|---|---|---|---|---|---|---|
| | s. | d. | s. | d. | s. | d. |
| Nottingham | 6 | 10 | 5 | 2 | 1 | 8 |
| Lincoln | 6 | 10 | 5 | 7 | 1 | 3 |
| West Hartlepool | 6 | 7 | 5 | 7 | 1 | 0 |
| Middlesbrough | 6 | 7 | 5 | 6 | 1 | 1 |
| Liverpool | 6 | 7 | 6 | 7 | Nil | |
| Leicester | 6 | 7 | 5 | 4 | 1 | 3 |
| Wolverhampton | 6 | 6 | 6 | 6 | Nil | |
| Swansea | 6 | 5 | 4 | 11 | 1 | 6 |
| Derby | 6 | 3 | 4 | 11 | 1 | 4 |
| Southport | 6 | 2 | 3 | 9 | 2 | 5 |
| Chester | 6 | 2 | 4 | 8 | 1 | 6 |
| St Helens | 6 | 1 | 5 | 0 | 1 | 1 |
| Newport | 6 | 1 | 4 | 0 | 2 | 1 |
| Exeter | 6 | 1 | 4 | 6 | 1 | 7 |
| Bath | 6 | 1 | 4 | 2 | 1 | 11 |
| Dudley | 6 | 0 | 6 | 0 | Nil | |
| Bury | 5 | 11 | 5 | 11 | Nil | |
| Worcester | 5 | 10 | 4 | 10 | 1 | 0 |
| Canterbury | 5 | 10 | 5 | 10 | Nil | |
| Wallasey | 5 | 9 | 4 | 6 | 1 | 3 |
| Northampton | 5 | 8 | 5 | 8 | Nil | |
| Cardiff | 5 | 7 | 4 | 9 | | 10 |
| Warrington | 5 | 6 | 4 | 11 | | 7 |
| Walsall | 5 | 6 | 5 | 6 | Nil | |
| Huddersfield | 5 | 4 | 5 | 1 | | 3 |
| Darlington | 5 | 4 | 4 | 8 | | 8 |
| Reading | 5 | 3 | 4 | 11 | | 4 |
| Ipswich | 5 | 2 | 5 | 5 (credit) | | 3 |
| Tynemouth | 5 | 1 | 6 | 1 (credit) | 1 | 0 |
| Burton-on-Trent | 5 | 1 | 4 | 10 | | 3 |
| Bristol | 5 | 1 | 5 | 1 | Nil | |
| Plymouth | 5 | 0 | 5 | 0 | Nil | |
| Portsmouth | 4 | 11 | 4 | 11 | Nil | |
| Southampton | 4 | 10 | 4 | 10 | Nil | |
| Blackpool | 4 | 6 | 4 | 2 | | 4 |
| Southend-on-Sea | 4 | 4 | 4 | 4 | Nil | |
| Croydon | 4 | 3 | 3 | 10 | | 5 |
| Bournemouth | 4 | 3 | 4 | 3 | Nil | |
| Barnsley | 4 | 0 | 3 | 10 | | 2 |
| Brighton | 3 | 10 | 4 | 3 (credit) | | 5 |
| Oxford | 3 | 2 | 3 | 2 | Nil | |
| Eastbourne | 2 | 11 | 4 | 7 (credit) | 1 | 8 |

TABLE B

Metropolitan boroughs and the L.C.C. Housing subsidies measured against debt charges for the financial year ending March 1963.

| Authority | Total subsidy | | Exchequer | | Rate | |
|---|---|---|---|---|---|---|
| | *s.* | *d.* | *s.* | *d.* | *s.* | *d.* |
| Stepney | 17 | 7 | 9 | 10 | 7 | 9 |
| Bethnel Green | 16 | 8 | 5 | 9 | 10 | 11 |
| Hackney | 14 | 11 | 7 | 8 | 7 | 3 |
| Southwark | 14 | 8 | 8 | 2 | 6 | 6 |
| Holborn | 14 | 5 | 6 | 5 | 8 | 0 |
| St Pancras | 14 | 4 | 5 | 6 | 8 | 10 |
| Poplar | 14 | 2 | 7 | 8 | 6 | 6 |
| Hammersmith | 12 | 11 | 7 | 2 | 6 | 9 |
| Bermondsey | 13 | 3 | 6 | 3 | 7 | 0 |
| Greenwich | 13 | 1 | 8 | 2 | 4 | 11 |
| Paddington | 13 | 0 | 9 | 6 | 3 | 6 |
| Stoke Newington | 12 | 11 | 7 | 10 | 5 | 1 |
| Westminster | 12 | 10 | 8 | 1 | 4 | 9 |
| Lambeth | 12 | 10 | 7 | 4 | 5 | 6 |
| Camberwell | 12 | 9 | 5 | 4 | 7 | 5 |
| Finsbury | 12 | 7 | 7 | 4 | 5 | 3 |
| Wandsworth | 12 | 6 | 5 | 7 | 6 | 11 |
| Deptford | 12 | 5 | 6 | 6 | 5 | 11 |
| Fulham | 12 | 4 | 6 | 3 | 6 | 1 |
| Battersea | 12 | 3 | 5 | 6 | 6 | 9 |
| Chelsea | 12 | 2 | 12 | 1 | | 1 |
| Islington | 12 | 1 | 7 | 11 | 4 | 2 |
| Shoreditch | 11 | 10 | 7 | 7 | 4 | 3 |
| St Marylebone | 10 | 7 | 7 | 1 | 3 | 6 |
| Lewisham | 10 | 6 | 6 | 6 | 4 | 0 |
| L.C.C. | 10 | 4 | 5 | 9 | 4 | 7 |
| Kensington | 9 | 7 | 7 | 7 | 2 | 0 |
| Hampstead | 8 | 9 | 5 | 8 | 3 | 1 |
| Woolwich | 7 | 9 | 4 | 0 | 3 | 9 |

*All subsidies given per £1 debt charges*

# *Index*